CAREERS IN
SOCIAL CARE

Bernard Moss

seventh edition

KOGAN PAGE

**YOURS TO HAVE AND TO HOLD
BUT NOT TO COPY**

First published as *Careers in Social Work* in 1980, by Anne Page
Second edition 1985
Third edition 1988, by Julia Allen
Fourth edition 1992
Fifth edition, reprinted 1995, edited by Elizabeth Atkinson
Sixth edition 1997
Seventh edition 1999

Apart from any fair dealing for the purposes of research or private study, or criticism or review, as permitted under the Copyright, Designs and Patents Act 1988, this publication may only be reproduced, stored or transmitted, in any form or by any means, with the prior permission in writing of the publishers, or in the case of reprographic reproduction in accordance with the terms and licences issued by the CLA. Enquiries concerning reproduction outside these terms should be sent to the publishers at the undermentioned address:

Kogan Page Limited
120 Pentonville Road
London N1 9JN

© Kogan Page, 1980, 1985, 1988, 1992, 1995, 1997, 1999

British Library Cataloguing in Publication Data

A CIP record for this book is available from the British Library.

ISBN 07494 2874 0

Typeset by Jean Cussons Typesetting, Diss, Norfolk
Printed and bound by Clays Ltd, St Ives plc

Contents

Preface v

1. Introduction 1
Is this the job for you?; Social care – what is it?;
Social care and faith communities

2. Getting started 6
Gaining practical experience; Some words about
disability – for everyone to read; Gaining academic
knowledge and qualifications; Things to read;
The importance of planning

3. Jobs requiring modest qualifications 14
Drivers; Hostels; Homes for older people; Other
residential work; Care assistants; ... and many more

4. Professional social work 19
Residential social work; Other settings;
Career opportunities; Postscript

5. Allied professions 26
Education welfare officers; Clinical psychologists;
Health visitors; Occupational therapists;
Speech and language therapists; Music, drama
and art therapists; Youth work;
Social care work in faith communities

6. Working in the criminal justice system 37
The probation service; The prison service;
National Association for the Care and
Resettlement of Offenders (NACRO)

Contents

7. Advice work, advocacy, counselling and mediation   47
Advice work; Advocacy; Counselling; Mediation;
Postscript: a note on salaried work with charities
and voluntary agencies

8. Gaining your qualifications   59
How to apply; Sources of finance;
Information about particular qualifications

9. Useful addresses   77

10. Further reading   86

Index   89

Preface

The list of jobs and careers in this rapidly expanding field seems endless. The good news is that there could be something to suit anyone who is wishing to pursue this type of career, providing they have the right qualifications and attitude. The not-so-good news is that this can be confusing territory, with lots of people chasing every vacancy. This book will help you chart your way through, and provide signposts and guidelines to help you make an informed choice, and prepare yourself as well as you can for a rewarding job or career.

In multi-cultural Britain it is important that the various care agencies reflect in their workforce the richness and diversity of the communities they serve. It is also important to recognize social care opportunities that are arising within various minority ethnic groups, and faith communities.

This book explores some of these issues, and is a useful starting point for anyone wishing to learn about this fascinating area of work, particularly:

- school- and college-leavers;
- people changing jobs or careers;
- people returning to work after a break;
- people wishing to enter the workplace at a mid-life point.

1 Introduction

Is this the Job for You?

- ❒ Do I enjoy working with people?
- ❒ Am I a good listener?
- ❒ Do I enjoy helping other people?
- ❒ Am I willing to undertake some training?
- ❒ Do I have a sense of humour?
- ❒ Do I respect other people?
- ❒ Am I mature in my approach and outlook?

If you have answered 'Yes' to these questions, then a career in social care could be right for you.

Further questions to ask yourself

- ❒ Do other people's problems upset me?
- ❒ Do I often get impatient or cross?
- ❒ Do I take other people's problems home with me?
- ❒ Do I tend to blame people for the problems they face?
- ❒ Do I tend to 'take over' when dealing with other people?

If you have answered 'yes' to these questions, it may be that a career in social care will not suit your particular personality.

Still more questions to ask yourself

- ☐ Am I deaf or hard of hearing?
- ☐ Am I disabled?
- ☐ Am I a wheelchair user?
- ☐ Do I find it difficult or impossible to see?
- ☐ Am I dyslexic?
- ☐ Do I find it difficult to get around easily?

The answers you give to these questions reveal important information about who you are, but should not prevent you from becoming a social care worker.

The field of social care will be greatly enhanced and enriched by more disabled people entering these careers and jobs. Of course, you need to be sighted in order to drive safely, and not every job will suit every disabled person, but in these days of increasing awareness and more comprehensive legislation about equal opportunities, you can be encouraged, together with everyone else, to explore an interesting, worthwhile career.

Don't be put off.

Social care – what is it?

At one level, we can easily list some of the career and job opportunities that come under this heading. These include:

- professional social workers;
- probation officers;
- prison officers;
- occupational therapists;
- speech therapists;
- health visitors;
- advice workers;
- care assistants;
- counsellors;
- education welfare officers;
- youth and community workers;

- hostel workers for homeless people;
- clinical psychologists;
- religious and secular workers in various faith communities.

Some of these jobs require lengthy training with previous experience before you can begin; others have less demanding entry requirements. For some careers you have to be over 21 or 22 to begin.

At a deeper level, it is worth reflecting a little about what it might mean to care for someone professionally. This is an issue you need to think about because it will help you understand a bit more about why a career in social care attracts you.

Generally speaking, if you are caring for people in a professional capacity, you need to understand the importance of respecting them as individuals who have dignity and rights. Care is occasionally something you do *to* people. For example, if you are caring for people who are severely physically disabled. More often, it is something you do *with* people, gaining their consent and working together in partnership – this is one of the buzz words you will hear more about in this field.

There will be occasions in some professions and jobs where you may have to make decisions or take actions against a person's wishes (for example, in child protection work, or in a prison setting), but it is still important to work in a respectful way.

The settings for social care vary enormously. These include:

- social work or probation offices;
- hospitals;
- hostels;
- drop-in centres;
- health centres;
- hospices;
- advice centres;
- residential settings;
- religious settings.

You may work a standard nine to five day, or be a shift worker in a residential setting. You may work for a local authority, a voluntary agency or a private organization. Whatever the setting, your role should be clearly defined and agreed by the organization. You should have a clear understanding of what the law says you can and cannot do in your job.

You should also have a very clear idea of what social care means in the agency you would like to work for, because it will mean different things to different people.

To illustrate the point, think for a moment what social care might mean for you as a worker if you are involved with the following people:

- a substance misuser;
- an older person needing home care provision;
- someone wishing to improve the quality of their relationship;
- a gay man being harassed at work;
- a child being abused;
- a teenager committing offences;
- a woman with children living in a refuge;
- a disabled person needing specific equipment or resources.

This chapter is really to help you to start thinking about some important issues in social care. You will want to take this further by reading journals such as *Community Care* and relevant books from the library.

You will also want to talk informally to people who are already working in the field(s) you are interested in. Ask them what is involved? What do they enjoy about the work and what gives them satisfaction? What frustrates them and gets them down? Build up a picture of the job to test out whether or not this really is for you.

Social care and faith communities

If you belong to a faith community yourself, you may well feel that a job or career in social care will be an expression of your religious commitment. If so, you will be in good company. Much of the impetus for social care has come from people of faith with a deep sense of social justice.

It is worth sounding some words of caution at this point, however. Social care work is important in its own right, and must not be used as a means of trying to persuade others to your way of believing. You will also need to be aware that at times your views and values will differ from those whom you are trying to help. It is important that you do not attempt, however subtly, to impose your values on them or to influence them inappropriately in their decision making.

The chapters that follow will give you further information about specific areas of social care, with an opportunity to hear from some people already working in these fields.

2 Getting started

Gaining practical experience

If you are:

- at school or college;
- planning a career change;
- returning to work after a break;
- joining the workforce after raising a family;
- completing other caring commitments;

the same point needs to be made. You are strongly advised to gain some first-hand experience of the sort of work you would like to undertake as a job or career. This is essential for some careers, such as professional social work, but there can be few agencies that would not regard previous experience in a prospective employee as a real advantage.

It is not always possible of course to get exactly what you want, but employers recognize this and will appreciate the effort you have made to gain some introductory relevant experience. Individual circumstances also affect what you can realistically take on, but the following check-list gives you a range of options to consider.

- Offer yourself for selection and training at your local Citizens' Advice Bureau as a volunteer.

Getting started

- Contact a local youth group or playgroup to see if they need volunteers to help (be prepared for a police check to be made to see if you have any criminal convictions).
- Approach local homes for older people.
- Many hospices have volunteer schemes to support individuals and their families.
- Your local Community for Voluntary Services (CVS) will have a range of opportunities available.
- Befriending organizations like the Samaritans or Victim Support regularly appeal for people to offer themselves for selection and training as volunteers.
- If you belong to a faith community, approach the leader(s) to see what opportunities they can offer you.
- Your local Probation Office may wish to recruit new volunteers to work with particular people under the supervision of a probation officer, or you may wish to offer yourself for selection as a prison visitor.
- Contact your local Advocacy Service – this is an interesting and relatively new aspect of social care.
- Go to your local library and browse through the list of charitable organizations in the reference library – this may reveal several local organizations crying out for volunteers.

Some words of warning

- You may be turned down – agencies have to select volunteers carefully, especially if they are to work with vulnerable people in the community.
- Some agencies require you to complete a training course, to ensure that you have the right knowledge level and personal skills to do the job properly.
- Being a volunteer does not mean being second best – you will be expected to achieve and maintain high standards in the work you do.

Some words about disability – for everyone to read

If you are a disabled person or someone for whom dyslexia is an issue, a career in social care is just as viable an option for you as for anyone else. It's just that there are some specific issues that need to be tackled to help you get the best out of your education, experience and training. This chapter cannot go into complicated details, but will raise some general points that are important for everyone, disabled or non-disabled, to consider.

Case Study

John is visually and physically impaired and recently completed a social work training course. He is now a disability equality project officer.

'Originally I was interested in social work as a job because I felt I would enjoy it and would be good at working with people. As a disabled person I found that restrictions were put on me regarding the types of jobs I could get and I found myself working in jobs I considered to be stereotypical and not satisfying. To add to this, I was finding that I was not being taken seriously in work. Unlike my colleagues, I was given unchallenging work; I was not expected to take part in training courses or to want a career, I was not being promoted. I guess some people would say that in view of the high rate of unemployment among disabled people I was lucky to get work at all. Nevertheless, I was very unhappy. I wanted and needed a change.

'I had a lot of concerns at the time that made the decision to apply for social work training difficult to make. First, I shared a lot of the same concerns, responsibilities and financial commitments as other mature students. Also like others, I had anxieties over my ability to do academic work. All of these concerns, however, were added to by the fact that I was a disabled person. Would the university be accessible? How would I get access to the books and course material? Would I be accepted by other students, and by other social workers while on placement? Would I get the support I needed? Would the admission tutors reject me because I would create too many problems for them? I had many questions in my head, but my determination kept winning through.

'I sought advice wherever I could, and through networking I managed to locate disabled social workers for their help and guidance. I sought advice on benefits, and joined a disabled people's organization called

ABAPSTAS (Association of Blind and Partially Sighted Teachers and Students).

'I went on to enjoy my training, both in college and on placement, but, sadly, I *did* encounter many of the problems I anticipated. Information was not always accessible; physical access was not always satisfactory; some people seemed to have negative attitudes, etc. I used a number of strategies to overcome these difficulties and I finally got through training, and then went on to study for a top-up degree.

'Today I am working with young disabled people as a disability equality project worker. I consider myself to be very fortunate to have found a job that may actually positively change things in people's lives. My training was a hard slog, but it was definitely worth it. I would encourage other interested disabled people to go for it, and not to let concerns get in the way.'

It is worth asking yourself for a moment what your reactions are to John's story. These could include:

- 'Isn't he brave – hasn't he done well?'
- 'He's exceptional – I couldn't possibly do that'
- 'Is it worth the struggle?'
- 'He's done it – so why not me?'

There are some important issues underlying each of these reactions. There are obstacles that prevent disabled people from making progress in their chosen careers, and it takes determination and, at times, courage to tackle them. There will be moments when you feel like giving up. John's story, though, like those of many others, can also encourage you not only to 'have a go', but to realize the potential within you for a successful career.

Dyslexia

This is the name given to a puzzling and wide-ranging condition that affects people's ability to process information accurately. For some people, it shows in their spelling or number work; others struggle to express ideas clearly on paper; some have to spend lots of time re-reading texts in order to understand the issues being raised.

Some further points make this a difficult subject to tackle:

- Not everyone believes dyslexia is a genuine condition – and this includes 'experts' as well as 'ordinary people'.
- Some people do not realize that the struggle they are having may well be an indication of dyslexia, and that help is available.

Case Study

Pat *is a student in higher education studying to be a social care worker.*

'For years I'd been struggling to make sense of words and sentences. People poked fun at me and called me stupid. I had to spend twice as long as everyone else getting my homework sorted, but I was determined to show them I could do it, and got two 'A' levels just to prove it. After a break I went to college, but then the struggle got worse until my tutor suggested I might be dyslexic. I nearly died when I heard that word, but I went for the test. When the results came through I was amazed. Yes, I did have dyslexia, but the report went on to suggest various ways of overcoming the problem. I even managed to get a really good computer with my additional grant, and now that does a lot of the hard work for me. When I put in my first big essay with the computer's help and got 65 per cent for it, I yelled so loudly with delight that everyone thought I'd been stung by a wasp. Dyslexia holds no fears for me now. Just watch me!'

Specialist help and resources are available for disabled people and those with dyslexia, both at college and in the workplace, but John and Pat highlight some good advice for everyone seeking a job or career in social care. Everyone can benefit, for example, from drawing up a personal profile. Ask yourself the following questions.

- What sort of work with people would you most enjoy doing?
- What help or support would you need to study and work more effectively?
- What are your strengths, and talents? What are you good at?
- What holds you back? What are your limitations?

Be realistic, but positive. Assume you can do most things unless there are good reasons to prevent you. In other words:

- *don't* assume you can't;
- *do* assume you can;
- *be clear* about what you need;
- *go for it!*

Gaining academic knowledge and qualifications

At whatever stage you have reached in your life, it is important to take stock of what academic qualifications you already have, or are working towards, and what you will need to achieve if you are to enter your chosen career.

This book, together with more detailed literature available from libraries and careers services, sets out some of the academic targets you will need to achieve. You will need to decide which courses are most appropriate for your needs, but among the many you can choose from are the following:

- *A levels* in: sociology, psychology, biology (essential for some careers such as speech therapy), law.
- *Access courses:* these are designed to help get people 'up-to-speed' academically. You can put together an interesting package of modules in the social care field, including topics such as 'an introduction to social care' as well as sociology, psychology, criminology.

A note to the unemployed

In 1996, the Job Seeker's Allowance (JSA) was introduced. It replaced Income Support and Unemployment Benefit, and has implications for those who wish to undertake voluntary work while being unemployed.

You need to visit your local Job Centre to gain full details, but, essentially, you must be actively trying to find work each week in which you are unemployed. This means that if you are undertaking some voluntary work as a means of preparing yourself to undertake a training course in social care, you must still be available for work.

The Open University (OU) runs a number of excellent modules in the social studies field. You can send off for a detailed prospectus for their Health and Social Care Courses (telephone 01908 653743). There could well be a course just for you, and you can gain further advice and guidance by contacting one of the OU's regional educational and training managers (for the OU's contact details, see the Useful addresses section at the back of the book).

Alongside these formal academic routes are the developments with National Vocational Qualifications, known as NVQs. These have become increasingly popular because they provide ongoing training and qualifications while you are doing the job. If you are already in social care work, the chances are that you will have the opportunity to work for an NVQ. Schools and colleges, however, offer a wide range of courses that introduce students to the NVQ experience. In some ways it is a complicated field to understand, because there are different levels you can attain. Some professional qualifications have an equivalent NVQ level – for example, the Diploma in Social Work is regarded as a Level Four, but this does not yet apply to every career or profession. It is worth exploring these issues at your local careers office to see how NVQs might best suit you in your chosen career.

Things to read

You are strongly encouraged to peruse the wide range of magazines and journals that deal with social care issues. *Community Care* is published weekly and is a magazine for everyone in social care. It gives a good overview of many relevant issues and has a comprehensive job vacancy section. For more specific journals relevant to the career of your choice, consult your library, careers office or a friend or colleague working in that field (see also the Further reading section at the back of the book).

The importance of planning

Underlying everything that has been said so far is the importance of planning. You need to gain clear information about your chosen career in order to make an informed choice. You need to explore what academic qualifications and relevant experience you should gain. Last, but crucially, you need to consider the financial implications of the choices you are planning to make. The funding for higher education, for example, is no longer available in the form of grants – far greater reliance is being placed on student loans. Seek advice from your LEA and Careers Office, or Job Centre.

3 Jobs requiring modest qualifications

The field of social care is so broad that we could almost say that there is something for everyone. For the jobs mentioned in this chapter, you will have to be suitable of course, and have the appropriate personal attitude and approach. Even if the 'paper qualifications' required are modest, you will still need to convince an employer that you are right for the job.

Some of these jobs may provide valuable experience for anyone wishing to move on to further training and qualifications. People considering job/career changes or wishing to start or restart work after a period of full-time caring commitments, may find these jobs a worthwhile place to begin.

There are dangers in this of course – some of the jobs described in this chapter have a high staff turnover, often because people regard them as stepping stones to 'better things'. This can sometimes mean that the quality of care given to people who use these services may suffer. It is important to stress, therefore, that anyone doing 'people-working' jobs needs to maintain the highest standards of care, dignity and respect towards those who use the services they are providing.

You should be aware however, that:

- these jobs are usually poorly paid;
- the hours can be long or unsociable;
- the promotion prospects are poor;
- you may be exploited.

Jobs requiring modest qualifications

When applying for a job, therefore:

- obtain a written description of your duties and terms of employment;
- find out who you will be responsible to;
- ask for a copy of the agency's equal opportunities policy;
- if you are going to work in an institution, ask to see round it;
- find out as much as you can about the agency before going for interview – it will help you feel well prepared and impress the employer who interviews you.

Drivers

If you enjoy driving and want to work with people, look for jobs involving transport. Social services departments (SSDs) and many other social care organizations require drivers to transport people who use their services. Sometimes this will involve driving specially adapted vehicles for disabled passengers. You will need a clean driving licence, and will probably have to complete some additional training. Agencies will also explain what the insurance arrangements are.

Case Study

Bob is a meals-on-wheels driver for a local authority.

'I wouldn't drive the van if I was carrying coal in the back. No, we are making contact every day with people who really need it, stuck alone in their houses for one reason or another, usually because they are disabled or very old. It is probably the only cooked food they get. We hear their tales and have a laugh with them, it's like getting paid for what you would want to do for people anyway. The reward is in the contact with them, the laughs, and when they say "thank you" you know they really mean it.'

Hostels

Most areas have a number of hostels catering for a range of needs. These include:

- accommodation for homeless people;
- bail hostels, run by the Probation Service;
- hostels for people with particular problems, such as drug and alcohol misusers;
- women and children escaping from domestic violence;
- people with long-term mental health needs.

These hostels are run by trained staff, but they often need assistants to undertake particular duties, which sometimes include 'sleep-in' responsibilities. Be careful: some hostels put far too much responsibility on untrained staff, and this can be very stressful, as well as being inappropriate.

Homes for older people

In recent years, the number of homes throughout the country has mushroomed, with private agencies establishing care centres to supplement the work undertaken by local authorities. There seems to be a continuing need for people to help in all these homes, whether they are privately run, voluntary or local authority ones.

Homes will vary depending on the needs of the residents. Some will require assistants to undertake a range of light general duties, whereas others will involve heavy lifting, washing, bathing and toiletting responsibilities. Some homes are excellent, with residents taking responsibility for various aspects of their lives and daily routine; others simply provide a basic level of care. Regrettably, some fall short of even the basic level, and residents have been neglected or even abused. Such incidents must be reported to the local Social Services Department.

Case Study

Susan works in a privately run home for older people.

'I came here straight from school. One week I work from 8.00am until 2.00pm and the next from 2.00pm to 8.00pm. We start by serving breakfast, then we clear up and make the beds. We help people to have a bath, and we are very careful to see that they don't slip. When you are on from 2 until 8 it's not so hectic, and there is time to chat to the residents. That's part of the job too, and that's what I really enjoy. It's what makes it really worthwhile.'

Other residential work

Residential care is also provided within the community for children, young people, and for adults with particular needs. Many large institutional hospitals have now closed, and smaller, community-based homes have been opened for people with mental health problems or learning disabilities, whom we used to call mentally handicapped. You may see jobs advertised for care assistants to help in these homes that have a wide range of responsibilities.

It is important to find out exactly what you will be responsible for, and to realize that not everyone in the community will be as tolerant and respectful as you are towards people whose experience of life is different.

One theme running through all such work is the importance of helping people enjoy their independence within the boundaries of necessary care for their safety. A lot of sheltered accommodation is now being provided for people to live as independently as possible, but with easy access to help and support when necessary.

Residential work with children and young people has frequently been in the news, with distressing examples of neglect and abuse. Standards and guidelines have been revised and improved so that everyone works within the spirit of the Children Act 1989. You need to be very clear about what you can and cannot do, if you are working with children and young people, and to make sure you are properly supported and supervised.

Case Study

Frances *is a warden in council sheltered accommodation.*

'I saw an advertisement in a local paper – "Warden wanted for sheltered accommodation". They were looking for someone with nursing experience, and I had that. Really what you are is a good neighbour – you are here for them and you are keeping an eye on things. I check that everyone is all right at least once a day. Each flat has an intercom cord. If I think that anyone is poorly, then I send for the doctor. I don't think this would be a job for a very young person – you have to be a bit of a stay-at-home.'

Care assistants

Local authorities are obliged to provide a range of services to help people live in the community as long as possible. This will usually mean that someone in need will receive a community care assessment from the local Social Services Department, and the person's needs will be clearly identified. These may range from receiving practical help with cooking, cleaning and shopping, to more extensive help with eating and drinking and personal hygiene. Care assistants may become involved in any of these tasks. Again, look in your local press and Jobcentre to see what is being advertised.

... and many more

As we said earlier, the list of jobs seems endless and we cannot mention them all here. Often schools look for people to help with particular tasks, especially in special needs schools. Play schemes need helpers. Many organizations require domestic and catering help; hospitals need all kind of ancillary assistants; doctors need receptionists. There could be something just for you. We hope you find it.

4 Professional social work

Q Why do you want to be a social worker?
A Because I want to help people.
Q What does 'helping people' mean?
A er ...

The hesitancy in answering that second question points us to some deep debates that have been at the heart of social work ever since it became a profession. This is not the place to go into great detail, but if you are considering a career in social work, you need to have some idea of what it is about.

The most popular and perhaps most easily understood description of a social worker's role is one that focuses on individual people who are vulnerable and in need. Social workers spend time listening, perhaps counselling, always trying to understand what makes people tick. Then they explore ways to help people make changes in their lives to tackle their problems more effectively. To help someone in this sense involves taking (for want of a better word) a therapeutic approach.

Others describe the role of a social worker differently, however. They will say that social workers can best help people if they make them aware of a range of resources and information that can help people improve their lifestyle. If someone can be helped to claim all the benefits to which they are entitled, and to make use of a wider range of community resources, that will be a significant improvement for them.

Still others argue that the sort of society we live in is fundamentally unjust and unfair and discriminates against people, particularly minority groups. Social workers, therefore, must be aware of these issues and be willing to 'challenge the system' and encourage people to take positive action to change society. Until society becomes more 'user friendly' for disabled people, for example, and recognizes their rightful and equal place in the community, the system will be 'stacked against them' and no amount of sympathetic social work listening and counselling will change that.

These are some of the debates you will enter into if you wish to become a social worker. You will need to be intellectually, emotionally and physically robust to deal with the pressures of being 'at the sharp end' of all the demands made on you. These demands seem endless as social workers deal with people right across the spectrum of society, as the following list demonstrates:

- adoption and fostering work;
- child protection;
- working with 'looked after' children and young people;
- people in hospital;
- people with mental health problems;
- homeless people;
- drug and alcohol misusers;
- people with learning disabilities;
- physically disabled people;
- hospice work;
- people in trouble with the law;
- people with senile dementia;
- families in difficulty.

Much of what a social worker has to do can be summed up in the word 'assessment'. People's needs have to be assessed, together with the risks they may pose to others or themselves. People's strengths and capacities need to be assessed. All this has to be done sensitively and in a way that respects people's choices and cultural backgrounds. You will find that social workers no longer talk about their 'clients' – today they refer to people as 'service users'. There is much more emphasis on consumer choice and citizen's rights, and social workers must respect these values. At the same time, however, resources are very limited, and social workers often have to make difficult decisions about what services can be offered.

Case Study

Ishfaq is a social worker in an adults' team in a busy city centre.

'One of the hardest things I have to do is explain to people that sometimes the money just isn't there – or that they don't qualify for a particular service. I often spend a lot of time talking to them in their own language, and they trust me to do my best, but then I come back and say, "sorry", and they look at me with dignity and respect, but in pain and I want to run away. But sometimes I can help people look at things differently and we can find resources from somewhere else in the community, and when that happens I feel ten feet tall.'

Other areas of assessment can often hit the headlines, and social workers must wonder whether or not they can ever get it right. They have a legal duty to investigate child abuse allegations, and at times have to remove children from parents in order to protect them. Social workers also are charged with the responsibility of supervising people with mental health problems in the community, and this sometimes involves assessing whether or not they should be compulsorily admitted to a psychiatric hospital. Risk assessment is a crucially important skill and, for these high-risk responsibilities, additional training is provided after you qualify.

Much of a social worker's time is spent arranging and organizing 'packages of care' for people who have been assessed. We have what is called the 'purchaser/provider' split in social care, and social workers often purchase care provision from other agencies. These could be specialist services providers for people with sensory impairments; or voluntary agencies such as Help the Aged or Services for Asian Elders; or it could involve organizations that provide care and support for people in their own homes. The arranging and costing of these care packages

Careers in Social Care

has led to the standing joke about no social worker being properly dressed unless a pocket calculator is carried alongside their ID card.

There are still social workers who are employed as service providers. This role occurs in the voluntary sector (such as those who work for NCH Action for Children or Barnardos) or in the private domain. Some organizations that work with older people or people with learning disabilities, for example, employ social workers. In the statutory sector, work done in family centres would be one example of a situation in which social workers provide an important service.

Case Study

Palbinder *works in a local authority family centre.*

'After gaining my Diploma in Social Work, I began working in a children and families team for my local authority. The work was fascinating and varied, and, after a couple of years' experience, I was allowed to take on some child protection work. Some of the examples of child abuse were really upsetting, but I felt it was important to have social workers who could do something to help, even if as a last resort all we could do was to remove the child from the family to guarantee their safety and protection.

'I was delighted when I succeeded in my application to join a team of social workers in our family centre. This is something I've really come to enjoy. Not that it's easy – we have families from several cultural backgrounds coming to the centre, and we have to be careful not to tell people what to do. It helps that I can speak several Asian languages – it puts people at their ease if English isn't their first tongue.

'Most of my work now is in trying to help parents become more effective as parents, and to help them improve their relationships with their children. They have sometimes developed violent patterns of behaviour that we try to help them change. It takes a lot of skill to understand why some people behave the way they do – but they can change, and we get a real buzz out of seeing a family beginning to make progress and to enjoy each other again. We know then that the chidren will be safe and develop really well.'

Residential social work

There are various settings where social workers can undertake significant work, such as day centres, residential homes, some hostels and hospices. The centres vary in their approach according to the needs of those who use them. A centre for people who misuse alcohol or drugs will have a different ethos from a hospice where you may be trying to help someone face their imminent death and to support their family. With other groups of people you may be undertaking social skills activities, and seeking to open up wider opportunities in the community, while in a women's refuge you may be exploring a range of options for a family escaping from domestic violence.

Other settings

You can find social workers in many other settings. In general hospitals, for example, there will be a team of social workers who have to deal with a wide range of practical, emotional and personal problems faced by patients and their families.

Case Study

Karen is a social worker in a large general hospital.

'I work in the medical unit of this hospital and cover five wards and a number of clinics. After the main weekly ward round when all the medical and nursing staff visit their patients, discuss their treatment, and plan what is going to happen about their discharge, there is a social meeting at which the social circumstances of a patient are discussed. An elderly patient might not be able to cope at home; a young mother whose illness might make it difficult for her to care for her family; someone is worried as a result of their illness or diagnosis. These can often be practical problems, but sometimes they are emotional or domestic problems. I think counselling is a very important part of our work – it is very satisfying to be part of a caring medical team.'

Social workers also form an important part of mental health teams, both in hospitals and in community-based settings. To get into this more specialized work, you will need to become an approved social worker (ASW), which involves additional training. You will work closely with psychiatrists, community psychiatric nurses and other professionals to provide a full range of services for mentally ill people. You could also work in specialized settings.

Career opportunities

Although there are still some openings for untrained workers in some SSDs, the key qualification is the nationally recognized two-year Diploma in Social Work. You may specialize in working with either adults or children and families, but, once you have gained your diploma, you can apply for any social work post that attracts you. The biggest employers of social workers are local authority SSDs in England and Wales, the local authority social work departments in Scotland and the Health and Social Services Boards in Northern Ireland. The greatest concentration of jobs is in the large cities.

Your diploma could also open up career choices in large national charities and voluntary organizations, the armed forces and various community organizations. The *Social Services Year Book* gives the addresses of all UK social service departments and other employers of social workers. You will find advertisements for posts mainly in *The Guardian* (on Wednesdays) and *Community Care* (a weekly magazine), but you should also keep an eye on your local press and any specialist journals or papers that deal with the issues that interest you (see the Further reading section at the back of the book).

After a couple of years' experience, you may wish to branch out or specialize. You will be encouraged to develop your own ongoing training and professional development, principally by undertaking post-qualifying awards (PQs). The modules for these awards may be provided by your own agency and a local university. Over a period of time, you can accumulate credits for a PQ award and an advanced award, as well as working for a degree. The systems can be a bit confusing, so check them out with your training department.

You may also wish to take students on placement, and undertake a practice teaching award to develop your skills in this field.

Most departments have opportunities for promotion. The senior practitioner grade has been developed for people wishing to stay firmly in practice as their skills develop. Others, however, prefer to apply for managerial posts, having perhaps undertaken some additional study in their own time for an appropriate qualification.

Postscript

Social work is a fast-changing, challenging, demanding and important service to the community. It places huge responsibilities on those working in this field, but it can be immensely satisfying, and enriching to both worker and service user alike. To do it well, however, you will need good supervision and support from within your agency, and the ability to do something different when you have finished work for the week.

5 Allied professions

This chapter offers a thumbnail sketch of some other social care professions to give you some idea of the range of work that is undertaken in the community. Those who practise in these fields have their own professional identity, title, expertise, skills and training.

Education welfare officers

Education welfare officers (EWOs) have the following responsibilities within both state and private education:

- ensure the regular attendance of students at school;
- help students make the most of the educational opportunities available to them;
- offer help to families experiencing difficulties that prevent their children from attending school or doing well;
- make resources available to families in need, such as free school meals, transport;
- liaise with other professionals, such as educational psychologists, social workers, probation officers, in order to provide relevant help to students and their families;
- work closely with parents, teachers, and allied professionals for the benefit of the students;
- contribute to the decision-making process for students with special educational needs;

Allied professions

- initiate court proceedings in extreme cases of non-school attendance.

EWOs work for a local education authority, and are usually allocated a group of schools in a particular locality. They take great pride in getting to know their schools and in being available to help in various ways.

The responsibility of ensuring that students attend school as a legal obligation means that EWOs can still be regarded as strict disciplinarians who knock at people's doors to find out why young people are not at school. However, many EWOs now regard themselves as education social workers who bring a range of skills and expertise into this arena.

Case Study

Narinder is an EWO in a city area.

'For me, being an EWO is both challenging and immensely rewarding. I like being on the move – my car is my office. I like having a "patch" to work and meeting a fascinating variety of people. Of course, we struggle at times with stubborn students who can't be bothered, but you would be surprised how often it is possible to turn things round just by taking time to get to know them and their family and to help them see things differently. I am sometimes the one in the middle who has to help both teacher and student adopt a different view of things, but most teachers welcome my help because they want all their students to do well. The hardest bit of the job is when I have to work with children who have been sexually abused, but fortunately I work closely with skilled professionals, like social workers, who do the in-depth work. But I still find it hard to accept that some children are treated in this way.'

If you would like to become an EWO, you should contact your local education authority for details. They are looking for mature, self-motivated people with an ability to work well with young people, and who are able to be part of a multi-disciplinary professional team.

Traditionally, many EWOs have had previous experience in other careers, but this trend is changing. You will need appropriate qualifications – the Diploma in Social Work is ideal, but your local education authority will advise you in more detail. The professional body is the National Association for Social Workers in Education (see the Useful addresses section at the back of the book for contact details).

Clinical psychologists

Clinical psychologists aim to develop a clear understanding of why people act, feel and think in the ways they do. They apply psychological theory and knowledge to a wide range of problems in order to assess, treat and support individuals and their families and carers.

Clinical psychology provides fascinating and rewarding career opportunities to work with a wide range of people in a variety of settings.

Clinical psychologists are not psychiatrists, and it is important to be clear about the differences between these professions. Psychiatrists are medically trained specialists who work with people who are mentally disturbed or unwell. Psychiatrists are able to prescribe medication.

Clinical psychologists are not medically trained, but have a thorough and prolonged training in psychological theory, approaches and therapies. They place a strong emphasis on the importance of assessment and work with the individual (and, if appropriate, family and carers) to come to a shared understanding of why a person is feeling or behaving in the way they do. They will then seek to work with the person to explore different options for overcoming their difficulties.

Clinical psychologists most often work within the National Health Service and usually with a particular client group, such as adults with mental health needs, children, people with learning disabilities. Although each client group experiences some specific problems, there are various common problems that clinical psychologists often work with. These include emotional problems, such as depression, anxiety disorders, recovery from trauma; mental illnesses, such as schizophrenia; addiction; sexual and relationship problems; psychosomatic and medical issues; and behavioural problems.

Allied professions

The areas of knowledge that a clinical psychologist would draw on include human development; understanding of cognitive processes, such as memory, learning; understanding human behaviour; how the brain functions; social psychology, and a range of therapeutic theories and approaches.

Clinical psychologists work with clients in a range of settings, including GP practices, in-patient wards, out-patient clinics, day-centres, schools and within clients' own homes.

Case Study

***Anna** is a clinical psychologist working for an NHS Trust in a city centre.*

'I love my job. It took a lot of study and effort to qualify, but it's well worth it. I particularly enjoy the variety of what I do. I work within a service for people who have learning disabilities, but the variety of things I do is huge. For example, in my caseload at the moment I am working with a severely disabled man to help him develop ways of communicating what he needs. I am also doing an assessment of an autistic child to find out what her memory and comprehension are like, to help her teachers plan how best to support her.

'Many of my clients have emotional difficulties and I often work with people who have experienced traumatic events. I am also working with a young woman who has an eating disorder, and a man who is so anxious that he behaves in ways that the other people at his day centre find difficult to cope with. I don't just work with individuals; often I'm working with parents and carers, or teachers and staff groups. Sometimes this is to support the individual client, but I run training courses for staff, too.

'The other aspects of my work that I find particularly rewarding are the research that I am doing and the projects that I am involved in with colleagues who work on the same team as me. I work in a multi-disciplinary team, comprising nurses, occupational therapists, speech and language therapists, care managers, as well as clinical psychologists. I like this because we all get to learn from each other – even if we disagree sometimes!

'The best thing about my job is the satisfaction of helping someone recover or get through a difficult or painful experience. But I suppose the down side is that sometimes there is nothing I can do to help, because situations are out of my control.'

How to become a clinical psychologist

You need a degree in psychology. University courses vary in their emphasis – some stress experimental approaches, and offer a lot of laboratory work; others focus more on social and developmental psychology. Go for the course you think you will enjoy most and do best at. This is important because you need to get an Upper Second or First Class Honours Degree.

Having gained your degree, you will need to acquire some relevant work experience. Many people do this by getting a post as an assistant psychologist. These posts are usually advertised in the local press and in the British Psychological Society Appointments Memorandum. However, it is often worth approaching your local clinical psychology service to explore possibilities.

The next stage is the hardest. Once you have gained a range of experience, you need to apply for a place on a post-graduate three-year doctoral course in clinical psychology. Places are limited (but gradually increasing) and competition is fierce, so you need to be determined and keep trying.

Once you have completed this course, you can apply for a job as a clinical psychologist in whatever field most interests you. There is a great demand for staff, and you will have the skills to make a real difference for people in need.

Health visitors

Health visitors have a nursing background, but the work they do has a strong social care theme to it. Their job includes:

- visiting people at home to assess their health care needs;
- promoting health in the community;
- trying to prevent mental and physical ill-health.

Health visitors are usually members of a primary health care team, including GPs, district nurses, midwives and others. An important part of their work is that of identifying factors that may contribute to poor health in the community, and raising awareness among people who can help to improve it.

Many health visitors focus on the needs of parents, especially mothers with young families, as they have a statutory responsibility for children from birth to the age of five. The health visitor will make home visits, and can advise on a lot of issues, from very personal matters to information about services available in the community. They may be the first people to suspect cases of child-abuse or neglect, and will call in social services departments to investigate.

Health visitors also work with older and disabled people, and at times have an educational role in visiting schools and colleges to lead sessions on issues like parenthood, personal hygiene, and sexual matters.

Case Study

Catherine *is a health visitor in a child development clinic that has close working links with a large doctor's practice. Before training as a health visitor, Catherine was a hospital nurse for several years.*

'I changed to health visiting because I liked the idea of working with families I could get to know over a period of time. Personally, I think it is a job for people with more life experience. I have a case-load of 400 children under 5. My time is mostly spent on home visits, on running ante-natal and post-natal support clinics, health education groups, and research projects. It is very satisfying to get a group running – it really is a case of a problem shared is a problem halved. My aim has always been to work in co-operation with parents and I think that, with experience, I have become more able to spot real problems, and know when something has to be done and when things are OK really.'

Opportunities

Once qualified and with two years' full-time practice, you can take further courses to equip you to train student health visitors, or to become a lecturer in health visiting studies. Courses are also available if you wish to pursue a management career.

Occupational therapists

Occupational therapists (OTs) have a broadly-based, medically oriented training, including hospital-based experience. They help people to achieve maximum physical, psychological, social and economic independence. Mainly they work with people:

- who are temporarily disabled, physically or mentally;
- with long-term disabilities;
- with progressive debilitating disorders;
- who have long-term psychiatric problems;
- who have learning difficulties;
- who are elderly and need their help.

OTs are usually members of a multi-disciplinary team with responsibility for medical care and rehabilitation. The main employers are the National Health Service and local authorities, but job opportunities are expanding into the prison service, and companies that deal with disabled people and the specialist equipment they may need. OTs can also become self-employed and work with individuals at home, in the community, in schools, work places and leisure settings.

What do OTs do?

The list can be a long one, and includes:

- working with young children;
- helping people with spinal injuries or burns;
- working in units for people who misuse drugs or alcohol;
- helping people overcome lack of confidence, anxiety or depression by encouraging them to undertake activities and projects;
- assessing disabled people's needs for personal aids or adaptations to their home;
- following through a treatment plan to aid ongoing rehabilitation;
- liaising with a disablement resettlement officer (DRO) to help someone find work;

- developing programmes of activities for day centres and residential settings to help people develop their independence and enjoy a stimulating environment;
- counselling and supporting recently disabled people and their families during a time of re-adjustment.

Case Study

Francesca *works as an OT for a local authority social services department.*

'After doing "A" levels, I worked as an assistant OT for a year to see if that was the career for me. The training is very broadly based and looks at the wider aspects of disability rather than just its physical effects. We have clients of all ages; the younger children would have conditions such as spina bifida or cerebral palsy. With adults, we see people with multiple-sclerosis, motor neurone disease, Parkinson's disease. With older people, it can be the general effects of ageing – arthritis, heart problems and strokes. Counselling skills are often needed on a visit; while we are giving practical advice, people find it comfortable to talk about other problems. But it can be distressing to work with young people who are dying fairly quickly, or people who are deteriorating rapidly. Sometimes I go and cry in my car.'

Opportunities

The prospects are good, and, as British qualifications are recognized by the World Federation of Occupational Therapists, it is also possible to find work abroad in affiliated countries. After qualifying, you can either choose a post that enables you to work on a rotational basis with different groups of people or you can go directly into a specialist area. In the NHS, there are several senior grades leading up to the post of occupational therapy manager.

Unqualified people can work as OT helpers or assistants under the supervision of a qualified OT in a hospital or in the community. You could be assessed in-post to gain an NVQ Level 3, as the College of Occupational Therapists is an approved assessment centre for NVQs.

Speech and language therapists

Speech and language therapy is closely linked to medicine, education and psychology. Therapists treat speech, language, voice and fluency disorders in people, including psychological and neurological aspects. People may be referred by GPs, consultants, teachers or health professionals.

The therapist will assess, diagnose and recommend therapy or other interventions as appropriate. Therapy may take place on a one-to-one basis or in groups. Fast evolving technology is helping therapists develop their existing skills very effectively.

This is a graduate profession and details of courses can be obtained from the College of Speech and Language Therapists (see the Useful addresses section at the back of the book for contact details).

Music, drama and art therapists

Music, drama and art can all be used in hospitals and day centres, both as sources of active enjoyment, and forms of therapy to help people communicate and express themselves.

There is professional training available. For more information, you can contact the:

- British Association of Art Therapists;
- Association of Drama Therapists;
- British Society for Music Therapists.

(See the Useful addresses section on pages 77–85 for contact details.)

There are also openings for unqualified people.

Youth work

If you are keen to explore a job or career in youth work, the chances are that you will already have become involved in some voluntary work with young people. The opportunities

Allied professions

for voluntary involvement are endless, from uniformed organizations, such as the Guides, Scouts, Boys Brigade and various Cadet Corps, to less formal groups, such as drop-in clubs, disco bars and helping out at local community centres or church halls.

Most organizations welcome additional helpers, but you must be prepared for careful scrutiny and a police check to make sure you will approach the work properly, and do not have any criminal convictions.

For careers in youth work, you would need to look, for example, to the Youth Service, which is usually provided on a partnership basis between local authorities and voluntary organizations such as the YMCA, Methodist Association of Youth Clubs, National Association of Muslim Youth, or the uniformed organizations mentioned above.

Youth workers appointed by such bodies usually enjoy a wide range of opportunities, working mainly with young people between the ages of 13 and 19. You might be based at a school, youth club or community centre; you might be appointed, however, to a particular locality as a detached youth worker, with responsibility for 'creatively loitering' among young people who do not wish to be organized or told what to do.

To be a youth worker, you need to enjoy the company of young people and be able to see the immense talent, potential and zest for life within them. However, you also have to be prepared to be rejected and treated with suspicion, and be clear about what behaviour you personally find unacceptable and will not join in. Young people enjoy challenging older people, sometimes to see how far they will go, so you need to know yourself well and to be emotionally strong and resilient.

Once you gain someone's trust, you may feel overwhelmed with the range of problems and issues some young people present to you. You may be the only 'listening ear' they feel they have; you may be the only person who takes them seriously; you may be the only one who will be willing to 'take their side' and speak up for them in difficult situations.

You will need to be willing to work unsocial hours, and to regard your career as a vocation rather than a series of lucrative promotion prospects.

If you are serious about wanting a career in this type of work, it is worth contacting a college that offers specialist training courses (see Chapter 7).

Social care work in faith communities

Many faith communities provide opportunities for paid leadership. This can sometimes be with specific programmes, such as day centres for older people; community service projects; drop-in and advice centres; young people's schemes and homeless projects. It is likely that payment levels for jobs in this sector will be modest, and the funding for such projects is often short-term, which means that workers can only be employed on short-term contracts. You should make sure, therefore, that you have as clear a picture as possible of the terms and conditions of the job before you accept.

Of course, you may or may not belong to the faith community that is advertising the job that attracts you. This should not matter, providing you are sympathetic to the aims and objectives of the organization. Equal opportunities legislation means that you should not be discriminated against in your application, although there are occasions where an employer may legitimately dictate certain aspects of the person-specification.

Another facet of paid leadership is that of spiritual leadership as a full-time career. Faith communities sometimes describe this as a vocation into which people are called and ordained, especially within the Christian churches. Spiritual leaders frequently become involved in social care work in their communities alongside the care they offer their members. Other opportunities include paid work in specialist settings, such as hospitals and prisons, industry and higher education.

Each faith community will have its own ways of selecting, training and appointing its spiritual leaders. If this is a vocation to which you feel drawn, you should, in the first instance, talk to a leader within your faith community who could advise you about the next steps to take in testing out whether or not this is the right path for you to take.

6 Working in the criminal justice system

To be a social care worker with people who have committed criminal offences raises more personal issues for the worker to face than perhaps any other profession. Whether you work in the probation service, prison service or a voluntary agency, such as the National Association for the Care and Resettlement of Offenders (NACRO), you will have to tackle some fundamental issues before you begin. For example, what do you feel about people who:

- steal other people's property;
- commit acts of violence;
- steal from shops;
- drink and drive and then injure people;
- commit sexual offences;
- defraud 'the system'?

The chances are that your feelings and reactions will vary in intensity – some offences will seem to be a thousand miles from your own set of values and code of living, but there may be other offences that are much closer to home for you.

If you want to help people who have committed criminal offences, what do you imagine you will be doing? If you are full of idealism, and think you can change the lives of people you will be working with for the better, this is probably not the type of work for you.

People commit offences for all sorts of reasons – people's life stories are so complicated and, at times, their freedom of choice may have been severely curtailed. The way some groups of people are treated within our society makes their quality of life much poorer than average. Some people make mistakes, others choose to break the law. Things are not straightforward, and to work within the criminal justice field requires you to be cold-headed as well as warm-hearted; clear-thinking as well as compassionate; a bit cynical as well as being committed to helping people to make changes in their lifestyle. You may indeed make a difference in someone's life, but it may not be in the short-term, and the immediate response you receive may be anything but warmth and gratitude. Ask yourself how you would be feeling if your situations were reversed and you were in trouble. Then ask yourself what you feel about punishment and how society should deal with people who commit offences.

The probation service

Probation officers are legally required to supervise and work with people mainly over 16 years of age who have been sentenced by a court for the offences they have committed. In fact, probation officers are involved at almost every stage in the 'career' of someone who has committed a serious criminal offence. These stages include:

- preparing a report (pre-sentence report, or PSR) for the court to help the magistrate or judge pass the appropriate sentence;
- being at court when the case is being heard – to process information and be available if called upon, especially if a place at a bail hostel is needed;
- staffing bail hostels for people sent there by a court, and working to help them change their offending behaviour;
- providing a service within prisons to deal with personal, emotional and financial problems brought to them by the prisoners; liaising with the 'outside world' and preparing reports for parole;

- supervising prisoners after their release from prison;
- supervising people sentenced by a court to community sentences, such as probation, or community service;
- staffing day centres, hostels and specialist services, such as work with sex offenders and drug and alcohol units;
- liaising with other colleagues and agencies to provide help and support with accommodation and job searching.

This broad range of responsibilities vividly illustrates the demands placed on probation officers. Many officers feel that, during recent years, the main emphasis of their job has changed considerably. They used to be able to spend a lot of time helping and supporting people on their case-load, using a wide range of social work skills. Indeed, probation officers regarded themselves as being primarily social workers in the criminal justice field. More recently, stricter requirements have been laid down nationally for probation officers' work. They are expected to supervise, monitor and control those who are on their case-load, and to take back to court any who do not comply. Many feel that this is a long way from their original motto of 'advise, assist and befriend'. Indeed, the Government is talking about probation officers confronting, challenging and changing offending behaviour, and recognizing that punishment is a central part of that process.

It is important to be aware of this shift in emphasis in probation work before you apply for a job. On the 'care and control' spectrum, there is an increasing emphasis on control not least because the service is responsible for supervising more and more serious offenders in the community. This is emotionally challenging and demanding work – not a career for the fainthearted.

Training

Training for probation officers has also changed dramatically, and this will have a great impact on recruitment. Probation officers used to train alongside social workers on the Diploma in Social Work courses. Most students were sponsored by the Home Office for the course, and the number of sponsorships each year was calculated in an attempt to ensure that supply met demand.

The whole system has now changed. People wishing to train as probation officers will no longer enrol on the Diploma of Social Work course. Nor will places be sponsored nationally. Instead, individual probation services, grouped together into nine consortia, will advertise for trainees, appoint the successful candidates, and provide the training. During the fixed two-year contracts for this training, each trainee will:

- learn to be a probation officer 'on the job' in the designated work place, and attain an NVQ Level 4 standard under the supervision of a practice development assessor;
- study for the newly created Diploma in Probation Studies at one of the new centres created for this purpose – the academic work will be to the standard required to achieve a BA degree.

During this two-year period, a modest training salary will be paid, and trainees will work a normal 52-week year in their workplace. On successful completion of the two years, the trainee will have gained a BA degree, a Diploma in Probation Studies and probation officer status. At that point, however, the contract expires, so the trainee will need to apply for job vacancies as they occur. There is no guarantee of employment.

These arrangements for training came into operation late in 1998, and are likely to take some time to settle down. You are strongly advised, therefore, to consult the Home Office Probation Unit, or your local probation service, for the most up-to-date information.

You should also bear the following points in mind.

- The probation service is going through a very difficult time, both in terms of adjusting to its new role and in reducing its staffing levels.
- The new training arrangements will result in two years' very hard work for trainees, who will be both 'in post' and undertaking a degree course at the same time.

◆ However committed you are, there is no guaranteed outcome for you after two years, so, although it may sound unduly pessimistic, you are advised to seek the best advice you can before embarking on this career.

A note about civil work

Probation officers have been involved with the work of the divorce court, as well as criminal work, for many years. At one stage, most officers undertook both types of work, but more recently, specialist civil work teams have been created. Their principal responsibility is to provide welfare reports for courts when there are disputes between divorcing and separating parents over residence and contact with their child(ren).

Officers also undertake some responsibilities for supervising contact arrangements in particularly difficult situations, and in some areas provide an in-court conciliation service to help parents reach an agreement.

This is particularly skilled and demanding work, for which further training is required. It is not clear at this stage whether civil work will remain the responsibility of the probation service or be located elsewhere following the major review of family court welfare services being undertaken.

Opportunities

The probation service remains a fairly flat organization in terms of promotion. Officers wishing to gain varied experience move sideways into court, prison, community service or hostel work. Training posts are usually at senior grade level. Senior probation officers are now 'middle managers' and to progress in this direction you would need to undertake management training courses. High-flyers aim for posts as assistant chief probation officers, and may hope to gain a chief probation officer post eventually.

Other work within the probation service

There are other opportunities for working in the probation service. Probation service officers (PSOs – formerly probation

Careers in Social Care

assistants) undertake a range of interesting and demanding duties, but at a lower salary level and carrying less responsibility than a probation officer.

The work can include:

- giving welfare benefits and debt advice;
- offering help in finding employment;
- undertaking court duty on a regular basis;
- working in hostels;
- providing help with prison visits;
- offering support to prisoners' families.

Most areas have several PSO posts, but competition for them is always very keen.

Case Study

Heather is a probation service officer in a busy city centre.

'My interest in this type of work stemmed from working in the careers service where I held a similar position. I worked very closely with a careers officer who had a specialist role of working with young offenders. I used to assist her with the group work she undertook at the local probation office. My interest developed from there, and I successfully applied to become a probation volunteer. Within six months, I responded to an advertisement in the local press for a probation service assistant. My experience stood me in good stead as I was appointed to the position.

'As much as it may sound "corny", the work appeals to me because I want to help people. Many of the people I meet are facing all manner of difficult circumstances following their appearance before the courts, so there is masses of variety in the work I undertake. The following examples highlight just some of the range of interesting tasks I undertake as part of my role.'

- Assisting probation officers with the supervision of court orders by seeing people in the office, or visiting them in their own homes, or in prison if they are serving a sentence.
- Working with people to make changes to their lifestyles and challenging their offending behaviour.
- Preparation of reports for court on individuals who have not been able to afford to pay their fines.
- Helping people with welfare benefit problems.

Working in the criminal justice system

- Liaising with other agencies, such as Housing, Benefits Agency, Social Services.
- Accessing much-needed resources for individuals, such as drug rehabilitation facilities, financial assistance and so on.

'Whilst in post, the probation service has funded my attendance at college to obtain the Diploma in Welfare Studies. More recently, I have commenced a National Vocational Qualification (NVQ Level 3) in Criminal Justice, shortly to be renamed Community Justice. This is now nationally recognized as the qualification for my job and other jobs at the same level within the criminal justice system.

'I have been doing this job for nearly ten years now, and I can honestly say that I still enjoy the work I do. No two days are the same. The variety of the challenges within the job is stimulating, and often satisfying. Of course, there are situations that I come across where no amount of assistance will ever change particular individuals, but that is where it is essential for me to maintain a well-oiled sense of humour.'

Community service teams also require mature people to supervise small groups of offenders who have to complete a number of hours' work in the community as decided by the courts. The supervisers are usually paid on a sessional basis, and in many areas they work at weekends, often on a Sunday.

Case Study

Ashfan *works as a sessional supervisor for a busy community service team.*

'I never thought I would enjoy it at first, because I got a lot of hassle being black, but once I had shown I wasn't going to be pushed around, things settled down. I have had a regular group now for several months, and we have decorated old people's houses and done their gardening. I think I know my group better than the probation officers do, and I can see how some of them are changing their ways. It affects them to meet some older people and to realize that burgling and frightening people really is scary. I sometimes think I do more good with these guys on a Sunday session than anyone else does in a month.'

Probation and bail hostels also require some additional staff to provide a range of general duties, including some sleep-in responsibilities. During the day, you would work with some of the residents to give them help, encouragement and support. You might be part of a group-work programme or have a particular responsibility to help one or two people who may need adult literacy, social skills or job-search advice and support. These jobs are under the supervision of the trained manager, but are not very well paid, and do not in themselves have career prospects.

The prison service

Regarded by many as the service that is at the sharpest of all sharp ends, the prison service, which has an administrative system for England and Wales, one for Scotland and one for Northern Ireland, aims:

> to serve the public by keeping in custody those committed by the courts; to look after them with humanity, and to help them lead law-abiding and useful lives in custody and after release.

Prisons are overcrowded by and large, and even the opening of new prisons in the public and private sectors has not improved matters as much as had been hoped. Some suggest that, like the roads, the more you build, the fuller they become. Major refurbishment programmes are being undertaken, however, to improve sanitation and general conditions.

Prison officers have a primary responsibility to keep prisoners in custody, and the regimes in the higher-category prisons are dominated by the keys on the chain. In open prisons, however, the regime is much more relaxed, with lower-risk prisoners being allocated to them.

Even where there is a good atmosphere in a prison, the work of the prison officer is stressful. Some prisons have high sickness levels among staff, which increases the pressure on everyone else. The work can be confrontational and dangerous as some prisoners can be very violent, and drug misuse by prisoners is a significant factor in many prison regimes. Some people with serious mental health problems are sent to prison because there is nowhere else to send them if they commit a serious offence.

Nevertheless, prison officers will try to build up good relationships with prisoners in order to create a positive environment, as well as trying to influence peoples' attitudes and behaviour. Many prisons have education and work facilities that need additional skilled people to come in and provide the services.

You will need to think about your own views and attitudes to prison and punishment, and whether or not you are comfortable in a strong authority role, before applying for a job in the prison service. As a career, it calls for men and women of integrity, humanity and leadership, with patience, humour and understanding. There will be times when you will feel scared, but many more times when you will be able to offer some significant help and support to a vulnerable prisoner that may have a profound impact on their future life. Many prison officers work closely with probation officers in prisons and perform similar tasks.

Opportunities

You can move around prisons to gain experience, then apply for various lower governor grades before aiming for the higher management positions. Salary levels are often enhanced by a lot of overtime payments.

National Association for the Care and Resettlement of Offenders (NACRO)

At the other end of the spectrum, NACRO works as a registered charity, devoted to developing more humane and effective ways of dealing with crime, and promoting the care and resettlement of offenders in the community. It runs programmes to help the victims of crime, and involves the community in crime prevention.

NACRO has over 100 projects and services in England and Wales. In Scotland, there is a completely separate smaller organization, the Scottish Association for the Care and Resettlement of Offenders (SACRO).

The charity does not have a career structure and often struggles with short-term funding that has to be re-applied for annually. This means that many staff work on short-term contracts. Most are recruited for their personal qualities, skills and experience, and receive training on the job. Many workers find the experience immensely satisfying. They feel that those who come to them for help and support regard them differently from 'official bodies', and a deeper level of trust and co-operation can be achieved as a result.

7 Advice work, advocacy, counselling and mediation

Grouped together in this chapter are four different types of social care work. Two of them are well-established – advice work and counselling – while the other two are relative newcomers – advocacy and mediation.

In spite of the differences between them, there are perhaps some skills and attitudes that are needed in all four types of work. You will need to be good listeners – active listening skills are a must. You must also be able to appreciate where someone else is coming from – what they are feeling and needing. Also, you must have a very clear understanding of your role and what you can and cannot do. Each of the types of work discussed in this chapter has its own distinctive approach, and each has very clear expectations of those who work for them.

Advice work

There has been a significant development in advice work in recent years, and in many ways it is a growth industry. The work of the Citizens' Advice Bureau is well known, but there are also other organizations and centres providing:

- housing advice, including black housing associations;
- debt advice;
- legal advice;
- advice for drug and alcohol misusers;

- advice for homeless people;
- immigration advice;
- specialist advice for minority groups;
- consumer and trading standards advice.

It is probably most useful in this chapter, however, to focus first of all on the Citizens' Advice Bureau, as this is by far the largest nationwide advice-giving agency.

The Citizens' Advice Bureau

This nationwide organization provides opportunities for full-time and part-time paid employment alongside the very large voluntary workforce on which it depends.

The Citizens' Advice Bureau gives free, confidential and impartial advice to all who approach them. They try 'to ensure that individuals do not suffer through ignorance of their rights or of the services available, or through an inability to express their needs effectively'.

The best way of getting to know how the Citizens' Advice Bureau work is to offer to become a volunteer, undertake the training in interviewing skills and gain the necessary knowledge. People come to a Citizens' Advice Bureau with all sorts of problems and enquiries. These may include:

- debt problems;
- benefits;
- disability issues;
- housing and tenancy queries;
- employment problems;
- immigration difficulties;
- racial and sexual harassment.

As a volunteer, you will gain general knowledge of many issues, but there will be others who specialize in particular aspects of the work – disability living allowance, for example, or representing people at tribunals. The Citizens' Advice Bureau has a comprehensive information system that is designed to provide accurate advice for most problems that come their way.

Advice work, advocacy, counselling and mediation

The paid work in the Citizens' Advice Bureau includes clerical and secretarial posts, but many larger Bureaux employ assistant managers and particular specialists on a full-time basis. There is a nationally agreed salary structure, and, once in the system, you can work your way up to becoming a paid manager or chief executive of a Bureau.

It is fair to say, however, that, in order to make a strong application for any paid post within the Citizens' Advice Bureau, you would need to have gained previous experience and a solid working knowledge of the field.

Case Study

Nishi is an Assistant Manager in a large city Citizens' Advice Bureau. She speaks several languages, including Urdu, Punjabi and Swahili.

'What attracted me to this job was the fact that I had been involved in a lot of voluntary work within my own community and I wanted something more. I needed the backing of a professional organization, which I got from the Citizens' Advice Bureau. I joined the Bureau as a volunteer and then became an advice assistant. My responsibilities at the time were mainly to advise at outreach clinics, which means that we take the advice to particular areas of the city, enabling people with disabilities, difficulties and so on to be in touch with us. Since becoming an assistant manager, my responsibilities have increased and my career prospects have widened and developed. I am now managing the Immigration Unit. I am manager of four volunteers, managing more outreach clinics, including an Asian women's clinic.

'I enjoy working on a one-to-one basis and seeing things through, so this is why I enjoy immigration work because it requires perseverance and enthusiasm. I feel that my enthusiasm comes from the time when I was a volunteer and did not want to be seen as a failure, and wanted to prove to my own community that voluntary work is valuable, and that you gain good experience for future career opportunities. Anyone wanting to get into this line of work would need to complete the NACAB training course, and also counselling skills would be beneficial, but, above all, the person needs to be impartial, and needs to appreciate and understand CAB policy.'

If you would like to find out more, the best way is to contact your local Citizens' Advice Bureau – the details will be in your local phone book.

Housing advice

In the housing advice field, there are opportunities in local authority housing departments, especially now that legislation requires local authorities to provide housing advice. In the voluntary sector, the work of Shelter has made a significant impact over many years. Also, the number of housing associations has mushroomed, and these provide career and job opportunities. Of particular significance is the work of various minority ethnic groups. The Federation of Black Housing Organisations provides a valuable directory of the work being undertaken. In the 1997/8 Year Book, Jheni Williams comments on housing elders from black and minority ethnic communities:

> amid the gloom of inappropriate or non-existent care over the last decade, black elders have hope through the efforts of a relatively progressive housing movement spurred by the fine example of black housing associations who have developed bright, imaginative and culturally sensitive sheltered accommodation.

Advocacy

This is a relatively new development in social care, but it is expanding throughout the country. As with advice work, organizations depend on volunteers, but there are increasing numbers of paid posts being created.

'Advocacy' means to speak out and act on behalf of someone else at their request. As an activity, it is very familiar to many of us – we may invite a friend to speak for us in a difficult situation; we may instruct a solicitor formally to represent us legally; we may ask a Citizens' Advice Bureau for help and one of their staff may represent us at a tribunal. People who help others in a professional capacity – like doctors, social workers, religious leaders, union reps – may all employ advocacy skills in their work when representing others.

Advice work, advocacy, counselling and mediation

In this chapter, however, the focus will be more specifically on recent developments in advocacy as a career. Although focused initially on people with mental health problems who needed someone to represent them, advocacy is now a significant force in work with children, older people, and those who are intellectually or physically disabled.

Advocates can often become involved in representing a person by challenging a local authority or social services department about the level of care they are providing. They may become actively involved in complaints procedures, because advocacy often becomes appropriate after something wrong has happened.

To be a successful advocate, you need to be able to:

- listen carefully, attentively and reflectively;
- clarify the other person's point of view;
- take your lead from the other person;
- put your views to one side;
- speak/write clearly and assertively on someone else's behalf;
- manage conflict when tackling people in authority;
- be honest;
- be independent.

Career choices vary considerably, and the best advice is to read the jobs page in *The Guardian* where advocacy posts are regularly advertised. As with counselling and mediation, some people combine advocacy with other jobs or careers. The overall picture is still very patchy, but some really fascinating jobs are beginning to become available.

You need to be clear about what prior experience is required. In children's work, for example, professional advocates need a relevant qualification and a minimum of five years' experience. The National Youth Advocacy Service (NYAS) was launched in 1998 and is developing its work steadily. Childrens' rights officers now have their own support network (CROA). Generally speaking, however, the work is still piecemeal, with some parts of the country making more progress in this field than others.

One of the real satisfactions of this kind of work is being able to make a positive contribution to a vulnerable person's well-being, sometimes by getting organizations to change. You need to be tough-minded, determined, have a committed sense of justice, and be prepared for set-backs. However, the job satisfaction can be immense.

Counselling

Counselling is perhaps one of the best-known ways of helping people, and many professions claim to use counselling as part of their work. Social workers, doctors, health visitors and many more often claim to offer counselling help as part of their professional repertoire of skills.

It is perhaps unfortunate that the term can be widely, and at times, loosely used. For some, it simply means listening carefully to someone in need; for others, it means helping people to explore in depth some emotional or relationship problems they are experiencing; for yet others, it is a very specialized therapeutic skill that needs years of training.

The British Association for Counselling (BAC) describes counselling as '... giving the client an opportunity to explore, discover and clarify ways of living more resourcefully and towards greater well-being'. Counselling is not giving advice – its aim is to help people to understand themselves better, and to decide what they want to do for the best.

Counsellors need to be able to build a trusting relationship with the person seeking help, and to ensure that their own feelings, attitudes and beliefs do not get in the way.

It is important to be warm, accepting, and not to sit in judgment over people. Counsellors are somewhat like mirrors, helping other people to see themselves more clearly before deciding what to do next. Counsellors do not tell people what to do.

Counselling often involves a lot of painful and difficult feelings, such as guilt, anger and resentment, that many people keep bottled up. To help people express these feelings in positive ways demands great skill from the counsellor, as well as considerable self-awareness. It is important that counsellors receive good, regular supervision.

There are many training courses for counselling throughout the country, from basic introductions to counselling, to those covering the more advanced stages. You can gain recognized qualifications – certificates, diplomas and degrees – and you can apply for recognition and accreditation by the British Association for Counselling, which monitors standards.

There are opportunities for counselling as a paid career, but you will need to have gained a lot of experience and the relevant qualifications first. You would need to develop your skills on a voluntary basis before being ready for part- or full-time employment. Counselling is a popular field and there is usually very brisk competition for paid posts, so most people combine it with other related work.

If you are interested in counselling people who are experiencing relationship problems, then you might want to offer yourself for selection and training with one of the marital and relationships counselling agencies. 'Relate' is perhaps the best known, and is the largest such organization in the UK. It provides comprehensive initial and ongoing training, with very experienced supervisors, and, in many ways, is an ideal grounding for anyone wishing to undertake a counselling career.

Although most Relate counsellors work part-time, on a sessional basis, many of them are paid for the work they do, usually on an hourly basis. Counsellors usually contract to provide about 120 hours per annum, to their particular centre. There are opportunities for very experienced counsellors to be employed on a more permanent basis, as supervisors and trainers, but the numbers of such full-time posts are low.

Case Study

Sylvia *works as a Relate counsellor.*

'Deciding to see a counsellor is a very difficult step for someone to take and I admire our clients very much. They come along to a strange room and see a strange man or woman and pour out their most intimate problems. The thing about a counsellor is that you are completely neutral and you are hearing both sides. You are able to show one partner what the other is saying. You actually see when you are successful; you can see it happening in the room, because, over the weeks, the couple will change. They talk more and more to each other; they are taking back responsibility themselves for what they are doing.'

Counselling experience can take you in fascinating directions and can open up many different career opportunities, especially if you have additional training, such as in management studies.

Counselling posts have now been created in many different settings, including:

- health centres and GPs surgeries;
- schools, colleges and universities;
- industry;
- voluntary organizations;
- private practices.

When you have gained the experience and the relevant qualifications, you can embark on a very rewarding career – once you have convinced an agency that you are the right person for the job!

Some agencies require people to offer counselling alongside other skills – counselling is only part of the work that is done. A good example of this sort of approach is an organization that deals with alcohol misuse, although there are many more, each with a different focus.

Case Study

Penny works for an alcohol advisory service.

'I am team leader at an alcohol advisory service, managing two of the teams in the county – one in the city centre, the other a rural outreach. I manage 7 paid and 20 volunteer staff. We offer advice, information and counselling to anyone worried about their own, or someone else's, drinking behaviour. Yes, it can be a stressful job, because the reasons for, and symptoms of, drinking to excess are often linked to a history of abuse and other trauma, depression and self-harm.

'I am a counselling supervisor and have a small counselling case load myself. I also co-ordinate the group work we offer. I am responsible for developing the service, recruiting and training volunteers, as well as giving presentations and health promotion advice to various groups from GPs to homeless people. I also go on local radio quite often. My work also involves chairing a forum for professionals in the alcohol and drugs fields, and negiotiating with statutory and other voluntary organizations over policies and funding.

'Before getting this job I trained as a CAB volunteer and then gained a Certificate in Counselling. I learn a lot from working with people and get satisfaction knowing that I am helping to prevent serious alcohol abuse in some, and promoting healthier lifestyles in others. Just a little change in someone's self-esteem is a success, and that helps me feel good.'

Case Study

By contrast, **Anne** *works as a manager of an independent voluntary organization offering support and counselling to anyone who is bereaved or is facing a life-threatening illness. As manager, she has to take overall responsibility for the organization's development and resources to ensure that it offers a high level of professionalism in the service it provides. This includes offering supervision and support for her colleagues. She also offers training and consultancy to other organizations and professionals, as well as undertaking some research.*

'I very much value being part of an organization that is at the forefront of its field, and which values and respects its staff every bit as much as the clients who come to us for help. My own experience has involved working in the voluntary sector for over 15 years, and gradually taking on work that had increasing management responsibility. I have undertaken an MA in Counselling Studies and Management Training with the Open University. Personally, I have found it extremely valuable to practise as a counsellor alongside being a manager, but this combination is not essential for the management role.'

Mediation

Mediation has become an important skill in many areas of life where disputes between individuals and groups need resolution. A 'mediator' is a skilled person whom both sides

Careers in Social Care

trust, and who is able to help the people in dispute work through a negotiated process in order to reach a mutually acceptable solution.

In the field of social care, family mediation is the best-known form – not least because it has been placed centre-stage in the new divorce procedures laid down in the Family Law Act 1996. Couples with children who are seeking a divorce will be strongly encouraged to go to a family mediator to work towards an agreed parenting plan for their child(ren) before the divorce is granted. Mediators will also help couples sort out a wide range of other issues, including property, finance and pensions.

Once the Act is fully implemented (in 2000 or shortly after), there will need to be a large number of mediators available to meet the increased demand that will exist for them.

To become a mediator, you will need to have relevant previous experience, such as social work, probation or counselling, or relevant legal training and experience. The most appropriate agency to approach for selection and training, if you have a social care background, is National Family Mediation (see the Useful addresses section at the back of the book for contact details), which provides a countrywide network of mediation services. In larger services, some mediators are paid full-time, but elsewhere they are paid on a sessional basis, in a similar way to Relate. The increased demand for the service in the years ahead, however, will eventually lead to an increased professionalism in the service, with more mediators being employed on a part-time or full-time basis.

Case Study

Roger *works as a mediator in his spare time. He earns his living as a social worker.*

'As a mediator I can't sort out a couple's problems for them or tell them what to do after separating, but I can provide a safe, encouraging environment to help them work out what is going to be best for them and

Advice work, advocacy, counselling and mediation

their children. Because it's a confidential process and not in itself legally binding, couples can explore options much more safely and creatively, and can try things out to see if they work. Then, once they have an agreement, they can check it out with their solicitor to see that everything is properly safeguarded. Obviously, not every couple can do this – extreme cases of domestic violence must be handled through solicitors representing each party – but you would be surprised how often couples previously at loggerheads do work things out. That makes my role very satisfying.'

The UK College of Family Mediators (see the Useful addresses section for contact details) is setting the standards for mediators, and developing the service to meet the increasing need for it. Its members include a number of organizations that provide mediation services throughout the UK.

Postscript: a note on salaried work with charities and voluntary agencies

If you like the idea of doing social care work in its broadest sense, but do not want to be swallowed up in a large bureaucratic machine, or to have your hands tied by red tape, a post in the voluntary sector might be just the right thing for you. Some of the jobs already mentioned in this book exist in the voluntary sector, too.

Charities and voluntary agencies cater for a very wide range of people who have problems of a social nature, and many of them employ full-time salaried staff, some of whom hold professional qualifications. There are posts for social workers, counsellors, occupational therapists, health visitors, administrators, information officers, publication staff and fundraisers. They all also depend a great deal upon the efforts of volunteers.

Some voluntary organizations also operate what are now called service-level agreements with statutory organizations – especially social services departments – to provide a certain level of care and support to people in the community.

If you decide to work for a charity or voluntary organization, you will be expected to provide a high standard of work,

57

but sometimes the surroundings can be cramped, especially in smaller, poorly-funded agencies. Many organizations are able to incorporate information technology into their administration, and several charities have benefited from larger organizations handing down computer systems when they have updated their own. Computer literacy is becoming an increasingly valuable skill in all types of social care work.

There is no nationally agreed salary scale for qualified employees, and salaries paid by charities and voluntary agencies are often lower than those in the public and private sectors. Annual pay rises may not be automatic, and pension schemes, sickness pay, maternity and paternity leave and pay, redundancy arrangements and rights to trade union membership cannot be taken for granted. Before accepting a job, find out as much as you can about these issues. The larger organizations are the ones that will offer the best promotion prospects; otherwise it may be a case of moving from one organization to another to advance your career.

For information about charities and voluntary organizations, consult the *Social Services Year Book*, the *Charities Digest* and the *Voluntary Agencies Directory*, copies of which should be in most public libraries. National, local and minority interest newspapers and journals will carry job advertisements, and there is nothing to stop you writing 'on spec.' to a body doing work that interests you to see what they can offer.

8 Gaining your qualifications

In the fascinating and complicated world of social care, there is a complicated and fascinating number of routes for gaining an appropriate qualification. In this chapter, these routes are painted with broad brush-strokes – for more detailed advice and guidance you will need to consult the appropriate advisers for the career of your choice.

Many of the careers outlined in this book call for a university education, and you need to familiarize yourself with what this entails. Depending upon your circumstances, you can choose one of several routes to a degree:

- full-time course – usually three years long in England and Wales, and four years in Scotland;
- part-time course – daytime or evening;
- distance learning – where you study mainly at home, such as with the Open University.

Some universities offer a professional qualification alongside an appropriate degree, but the onus is on you to choose what suits you best for the career of your choice.

These days, degrees are designed on a modular system with credits awarded for each component or module of the degree. You need 120 credits in each of your three years of study to gain an Honours degree. Many courses allow a good choice of options to accompany the core modules of the degree, so that you can construct a highly relevant qualification. If, however, you enrol on a course that is the gateway to a professional qualification – such as a Diploma in Social Work or Probation Studies – most, if not all, modules will be predetermined and compulsory because they cover the core subjects for that particular career.

Although this chapter will give you some basic signposts for finding your way around, you should also consult more detailed reference books for the career of your choice, either at your local library or careers service, and the careers staff who are there to discuss matters with you in detail.

How to apply

Admissions to colleges and universities (for first degree courses) are handled by the Universities and Colleges Admission Service (UCAS; see the Useful addresses section at the back of the book for contact details). You place your choices in order of priority, and then send in your forms a year in advance to UCAS. Part-time and higher degree applications, however, are made direct to the university of your choice. For some courses, such as social work, you make an application via a separate body (see below).

You are strongly advised to attend any open days run by universities offering courses that interest you. This will help you to get the feel of the place, meet some staff and ask questions. This is particularly important if you are a disabled student.

After the paperwork is sent in, it will be sent to the universities and colleges in descending order of priority. You will hear from them as to whether or not they are offering you a place, and whether or not the offer is unconditional or conditional upon gaining certain grades at 'A' level or equivalent.

Many universities and colleges have policies to attract older students and may be willing to offer you a place if they feel you can do well, even though you may not meet the exact entry requirements.

Sources of finance

With increasing numbers of students going into higher education, the costs to the Government have been escalating. Changes that have been made to the funding of higher education as a result will affect most students. In basic terms, the student grant, which previously was paid by local education authorities to cover tuition fees, maintenance and other costs, has been drastically cut back. Many students have to pay £1000 at the start of their course, and take out student loans for the rest of their expenses, which you pay back over a period of years once you are in a reasonably paid job. For exact details, contact your local education authority. Disabled students will still qualify for the Disabled Students' Allowance, but, again, you need to contact your local education authority for detailed information.

Other forms of financial support have also disappeared, including bursaries for postgraduate social work training, and Home Office sponsorship for probation training. Some organizations still second some of their employees for further training and education. In the past, social services departments used to second staff on to full-time courses to gain their Diploma in Social Work, but this trend is changing. Secondments have been channelled into part-time routes so that workers can maintain a workload within the agency while completing their course. It is likely, however, that, with the development of open and distance learning, Accredited Prior Learning (APL) and Accredited Prior Experiential Learning (APEL) schemes, the pattern of secondments may change still further, with the Open University Diploma in Social Work proving popular with some employers. So, the days of being a salaried, seconded student, the envy of your colleagues, may be over.

If all of this sounds gloomy, it is not meant to be discouraging. A university education is still immensely rewarding and a sound investment, but you need to count the cost financially from the outset, both personally and together with your family, your partner and those most closely involved. (This may include your bank manager if you have one). More and more students are working part-time or on a casual basis in order to make ends meet.

Other sources of funding include trusts or charities. If you are unable to obtain any funding from statutory sources, it is worth contacting the Educational Grants Advisory Service at the Family Welfare Association for information advice (see the Useful addresses section at the back of the book for contact details). Also, you can consult the following books in your local library:

- *Directory of Grant Making Trusts* (Charities Aid Foundation);
- *Grants Register* (Macmillan);
- *Charities Digest* (Family Welfare Association).

Useful tips

Some colleges and universities waive their fees for part-time students. Most colleges and universities have hardship funds, *but* you will probably need to have taken out a student loan already and these funds are usually for particular emergencies and hardship so only modest payments are made.

Information about particular qualifications
Social work

At the time of writing, the ultimate responsibility for the training of social workers still rests with Central Council for Education and Training in Social Work (CCETSW). The Diploma in Social Work is the two-year programme of academic study and assessed placement experience designed to equip you to begin a career in professional social work.

The future of social work training, however, is far from clear. The government plans to abolish CCETSW and replace it with a new Training Organisation for the Personal Social Services (TOPSS), which is due to start work in January 2000. The details of this are still not clear. Social work itself is under review, and, structurally, the responsibilities of social workers and people working in the health service *may* be brought

Gaining your qualifications

together in one new government department. The providers of social work training are exploring different ways of delivering their service. Alongside the 'traditional' part- and full-time courses at colleges and universities, there are other routes being developed that help people already working in the field gain at least the first year of their Diploma in Social Work in their workplace.

In these uncertain times, all we can advise you to do is 'watch this space' and tell you what the situation is at the time of writing. For more detailed information, contact the CCETSW and ask for their handbook on Diploma in Social Work courses (see the Useful addresses section on pages 77–85 for the office for your area).

Application procedures
Most non-graduate and post-graduate programmes recruit via the Social Work Admissions System (SWAS). You should send your completed form to SWAS by mid December, with the registration fee (see the Useful addresses section on pages 77–85 for contact details).

Late applications (that is, those made from January to May) will still go to SWAS, but will be forwarded only to those programmes that still have vacancies.

Undergraduate programmes recruit through the Universities and Colleges Admissions Services (UCAS). Again, the closing date for applications is mid-December. For full details, including application forms, contact UCAS at the address given in the Useful addresses section at the back of the book.

Details of courses
Key

E Employment-based programme. Students are already employed in the personal social services when they apply for admission to a course, with the agreement of their employer. They keep their jobs and continue to be paid a salary.

DO College has a distance/open learning course.

Co College-based programme. Students are supported by LEA grants, student loans, bursary or private means.

CJ Criminal Justice course offered.

D College has facilities for disabled students.

NG, PG, UG Courses designed for non-graduates, (NG), graduates (PG) or undergraduates (UG).

Note that some programmes for graduates accept non-graduates, and some non-graduate programmes accept graduates. This is especially true for employment-based programmes.

PT These programmes offer a part-time route.

C There is a system in place for credit accumulation and transfer (CATS) whereby previous academic study may bring exemption from part of the programme.

Top-up The programme provides an option to obtain a degree by means of further study in addition to the Diploma in Social Work.

A The course offers accreditation of prior experiential learning (APEL), which may bring exemption from some part of the programme.

Aberdeen
North of Scotland Consortium
The Robert Gordon University
NG route, Co, DO, PT, D, C, A
UG route, Co, D, C
PG route, Co, CJ, D, C
Northern College, Aberdeen
NG route, E, Co, DO, CJ, PT, D, C,A

Antrim
Northern Ireland Diploma in Social Work
Employment-based route, E, NG, D

Bangor
North and West Wales Training Consortium
University of Wales
PG route, Co
Coleg Menai
NG route, Co

Bath
University of Bath and Partners
UG route, Co, CJ, D

Belfast
Queens University Education and Social Services Training Partnership. (QUEST)
PG route, Co, D

Birmingham
Birmingham and West Midlands Partnership
Diploma in Social Work NG route, Co, UG, PT, C, A, top up, D
Selly Oak Colleges
NG route, Co, top up, D, C
University of Birmingham
PG route, Co

Bournemouth
Employment-based route, NG, D

Bradford
UG course, Co, D, C

Brighton
East Sussex
Employment-based route, Co, NG, D
University of Sussex
PG route, Co, CJ, D, C

Bristol
University of the West of England, Bristol and Partners
Employment-based route, NG, PT, top up, D, C, A
Bristol University and Partners
UG and NG route, Co, top up, D
PG route, Co, D

Bromsgrove
West Midlands
Diploma in Social Work, Employment-based route, Co, NG, PT, top up, D

Canterbury
Kent Consortium – Canterbury Christ Church College
NG route, Co, top up D, A

Cardiff
South Wales
Diploma in Social Work, employment-based route, Co, NG, top up, D
University of Wales, College of Cardiff Consortium, PG route, Co, D

Chatham Kent Consortium
Mid Kent College
NG route, Co, D, A

Cheltenham
Gloucestershire Partnership
Employment-based route, Co, NG, D,C,A

Chichester
West Sussex
Diploma in Social Work, employment-based route, Co, NG, D

Coventry
Coventry University
Employment-based route, Co, UG, PT, D, C, A
Warwick University
PG route, Co, D

Derby
University of Derby
PG, NG, UG routes, Co, PT, D

Gaining your qualifications

Dundee
University of Dundee
UG route, Co, CJ, D
PG route, Co, CJ, D
Northern College (Dundee Campus and Partners)
NG route, Co, CJ, top up, D, C, A

Durham
University of Durham
Employment-based route, Co, CJ, D, PG route
New College, Durham
Employment-based route, Co, NG, D, C

Edinburgh
University of Edinburgh
PG route, Co, CJ, D
Moray House Institute/Heriot-Watt University
UG route, Co, D, C, A
Lothian and Borders Training Consortium
Employment-based route, Co, NG, D

Essex
Anglia Consortium
Employment-based route, Co, NG, PT, top up, C, A

Exeter
Exeter University and Devon Programme Providers
PG route, Co, D

Glasgow
University of Strathclyde
UG route, Co
Glasgow Caledonian
UG route, Co, CJ
PG route, Co, D
University of Glasgow
PG route, Co, D
Longside College of FE and Clydebank College of FE
Employment-based route, NG, A

67

Hatfield
University of Hertfordshire Consortium
UG route, Co, top up, D, A

High Wycombe
Buckinghamshire
Diploma in Social Work, NG and UG routes, Co, PT, D, C, A

Huddersfield
University of Huddersfield
UG route, Co, D, C, A

Hull
University of Lincolnshire and Humberside
Employment-based route, Co, NG, UG, D, C
University of Hull
UG route, Co, D
PG route, Co, D, C

Ilkley
West Riding, Bradford and Ilkley College
Diploma in Social Work, employment-based route, Co, NG, UG, D, C

Ipswich
Suffolk/Essex Consortium
NG route, Co, D, C

Jordanstown
University of Ulster at Jordanstown
NG route, Co, CJ, D, C

Keele
Keele University
PG route, Co, CJ

Gaining your qualifications

Lancaster
Lancaster University
UG route, Co, D
PG route, Co, top up, D

Leeds
Diploma in Social Work, NG route, Co, D, C, A
PG route, Co, D, C, A

Leicester
De Montfort University
UG route, Co, CJ, D, C
University of Leicester
PG route, Co, CJ, D

Liverpool
Merseyside Diploma in Social Work, PG and UG routes, Co, CJ, D
University of Liverpool Consortium
PG route, Co, CJ, D

London
(Greater London)
Goldsmith's Consortium
PG route, Co, D
Kingston
Diploma in Social Work/BA, UG route, Co, CJ, C
Middlesex University
UG route, Co, CJ, PT, C
PG route, Co, CJ, C, A
North-East London (Havering)
Employment-based route, Co, NG, D, C, A
East London Consortium
Employment-based route, Co, NG, D
North London Consortium – University of North London
NG and UG routes, Co, PT, top up, D, C, A
London and South-West Thames
PG route, Co
South Bank University

PG route, Co, top up, D, C
South East London
UG route, Co
South East (Bromley)
Employment-based route, Co, NG, PT, D
West London
Employment-based route, NG, DO, PT, C
UG route, Co, CJ, C
PG route, Co, CJ, C

Londonderry
University of Ulster, Magee College
UG and PG routes, Co, CJ, D, C

Luton
Bedfordshire
Diploma in Social Work, NG route, Co, top up, D, C, A

Manchester
Manchester University Partnership
PG and NG routes, Co, CJ, top up, D
Manchester Metropolitan Partnership
PG and NG routes, Co, top up, D

Middlesborough
Teeside Partnership
NG route, Co, PT, D, C, A

Milton Keynes
NG route, Co, CJ, PT, D, C

Newcastle upon Tyne
NG route, Co, top up, D, C, A

Northampton
Employment-based route, Co, NG, PT, D, C

Norwich
Norfolk
Diploma in Social Work,
NG route, Co, PT, D, C
University of East Anglia
PG route, Co, D

Nottingham
Nottingham Trent University
NG route, Co, CJ, PT, top up C, A
University of Nottingham
PG route, Co, D

Oxford
University of Oxford
PG route, Co, PT, D
Oxford Brookes
NG route, Co, PT, D, C, A
Ruskin College
NG route, Co

Paisley
West of Scotland Consortium
University of Paisley
UG route, Co, D

Plymouth
University of Plymouth
UG route, Co, D, C

Portsmouth
Employment-based route, Co, NG, top up, D, C

Preston
North-West England
PG and NG routes, Co, PT, top up, D, C

Reading
Bracknell and Wokingham College
Employment-based route, NG, PT
University of Reading
PG route, Co, D

Redruth
NG route, Co, PT, top up, D, C

Salford
Employment-based route, Co, D, O, PG, UG, NG, top up, D, C, A

Sheffield
Sheffield Hallam University
UG route, Co, PT, D, C
Sheffield University
PG route, Co, D

Southampton
University of Southampton
PG and UG routes, Co, D, C
Hampshire Consortium
Employment-based route, NG, top up, D

Stirling
University of Stirling and Partners
PG and UG routes, Co, D

Stockport
Employment-based route, Co, NG, UG, PT, D, C, A

Stoke on Trent
Staffordshire University
NG route, Co, PT, top up, D

Sunderland
University of Sunderland
UG route, Co, C, A

Swansea
University College
PG route, Co, D

Telford
Employment-based route, Co, NG

Tiverton
Employment-based route, Co, NG, D

Trowbridge
NG route, Co, D, C

Wakefield
Employment-based route, Co, NG, D

Wrexham
North East Wales Institute
NG route, Co, D

York
PG route, Co, D

Post-qualifying education and training
CCETSW has established a new framework for the continuing professional development of qualified social workers. There are two new awards – the post-qualifying award and the advanced award.

The post-qualifying award (PQSW) builds on the standards of the Diploma in Social Work and is designed to recognize the skills and expertise of social work. The advanced award (AASW) is a qualification recognizing high-level skills of practice in social work, policy making, leadership and management.

The post-qualifying framework (PQ) is based on a system of credit accumulation and transfer (CATS) and on the assessment of a social workers' practice competence as the result of their learning. The PQ framework is implemented by consortia formed by local collaborations of agencies and educational institutions. CCETSW approves and monitors the work of the consortia to ensure that high standards and consistency are maintained.

The awards are open to social workers with a Diploma in Social Work, CQSW, CSS qualifications or equivalent. It is necessary to register with your local consortium. A free PQ information pack is available from CCETSW (see the Useful addresses section on pages 77–85).

Education welfare officers

If you are considering this as a first career, you should apply for a social work training course and gain the Diploma in Social Work. You could possibly undertake some of your placement experience in an education welfare setting, and some courses offer a specialist educational option.

If you are considering a career change, then it is worth discussing this with your local principal education welfare officer. Experience and general maturity are important qualifications, and many educational welfare officers have moved into this work from other occupations. Training courses are available, sometimes on a day-release basis to bring you 'up to speed'.

Clinical psychology

See pages 28–30 for the qualifications required. For further details, contact the British Psychological Society (the address and other contact details are given in the Useful addresses section at the back of the book).

The probation service

Following the re-structuring of probation training, nine consortia have been formed for the selection and training of probation officers. If you require details, you need to send an A4 self-addressed envelope (with stamps to the value of £1) to the consortium covering the area in which you hope eventually to work. You will then be sent full details of the course and selection procedures (for consortia addresses, see the Useful addresses section at the back of the book).

Advice work

For selection and training with the Citizens Advice Bureau, ring your local CAB Bureau for details. The national training component is arranged through the local Bureau.

There are some courses available that you could explore for an academic qualification. Staffordshire University offers a Diploma in Advice Work and Law, with a placement in an advice work agency to gain valuable experience. The two-year diploma course can lead on to either a Bachelor of Laws (LLB) degree or a BA in Applied Social Studies (see the Useful addresses section at the back of the book for contact details for Staffordshire University). For further details about advice work agencies, contact the Federation of Independent Advice Centres (FIAC) (again, contact details can be found in the Useful addresses section).

Counselling

For details of careers, training and accreditation, contact the British Association for Counselling (BAC), which is the national professional accrediting agency (see the Useful addresses section at the back of the book).

Many further and higher education colleges and universities have counselling and counselling skills courses at introductory, certificate and diploma levels. Some offer Masters degrees. Most of the courses are run on a part-time basis for people in the locality. Contact your nearest college or university for details. The BAC also produces a survey of postgraduate courses in counselling.

Mediation training for people with social work backgrounds is offered by National Family Mediation (NFM). Contact your local counselling service or write direct to NFM for details (see the Useful addresses section at the back of the book for contact details).

Marital and couple counselling training is offered by Relate, and Marriage Care (formerly the Catholic Marriage Advisory Council). Their selection and training procedures are very similar. You need to be selected by them – they assess whether or not you have the appropriate qualities to be a counsellor – and then sponsored by your local service.

Training takes place at the national training centres over a period of two years or more on a modular residential basis. Supervision of all counselling work is very important, and so, during training, counsellors are required to keep a personal journal that records the process of development and learning.

A formal certificate in marital and couple counselling is awarded after candidates have successfully completed the stringent training and a further 400 supervised counselling hours.

Contact the Training Officer at Relate and/or Marriage Care for further details (see the Useful addresses section at the back of the book for contact details).

Youth work

The following colleges offering specialist training courses.

Bradford and Ilkley – Youth and Community Development
De Montfort University – Youth and Community Development
Leeds Metropolitan University – Community and Youth Studies
Manchester Metropolitan University – Youth and Community Studies
Oxford Brookes University – Youth and Community and Applied Theology
Reading University – Youth and Community Studies
University College of St Martin (Lancaster and Cumbria) – Youth and Community Studies

9 Useful addresses

Association of Blind & Partially Sighted Teachers and Students, (ABAPSTAS), BM Box 6727, London WC1N 3XX; Tel: 01484 517954

Association of Community Workers, Grindon Lodge, Beech Grove Road, Newcastle upon Tyne NE4 2RS; Tel: 0191 272 4341

British Association of Art Therapists, 11a Richmond Road, Brighton, East Sussex BN2 3RL

British Association of Counselling (BAC), 1 Regent Place, Rugby CV21 2PJ; Tel: 01788 550899

British Association of Drama Therapists, 41 Broomhouse Lane, Hurlingham Park, London SW6 3DP

British Association of Social Workers, 16 Kent Street, Birmingham B5 6RD; Tel: 0121 622 3911

British Council of Disabled People (BCDP), Litchurch Plaza, Litchurch Lane, Derby DE24 8AA; Tel: 01332 295551, Fax: 01332 295580, Textphone: 01332 295581

British Dyslexia Association, 98 London Road, Reading, Berkshire RG1 5AU; Tel: 01189 662677, Fax: 01189 351927, Helpline: 01189 668271

British Psychological Society, St Andrews House, 48 Princess Road East, Leicester LE1 7DR; Tel: 0116 254 9568, Fax: 0116 247 0787, e-mail: enquiry@bps.org.uk

British Society for Music Therapy, 25 Rosslyn Avenue, East Barnet, Hertfordshire EN4 8DH; Tel: 0181 368 8879

Central Council for Education and Training in Social Work (CCETSW) offices, Bursaries Office, 3rd Floor, Caledonian House, 223–231 Pentonville Road, London N1 9NG; Tel: 0171 833 2524

Central Office, Derbyshire House, St Chad's Street, London WC1 8AD; Tel: 0171 278 2455

London and South East England, Caledonian House, 223–231 Pentonville Road, London N1 9NG; Tel: 0171 833 8090

Thames Valley and South West England, 58 Royal York Crescent, Clifton, Bristol BS8 4JP; Tel: 0117 973 4137

Central England, Myson House, Railway Terrace, Rugby CV21 3HT; Tel: 01788 572119

Northern England, 26 Park Row, Leeds LS1 5QB; Tel: 0113 243 1516

Northern Ireland, 6 Malone Road, Belfast BT9 5BN; Tel: 01232 665390

Scotland, 5th Floor, 78/80 George Street, Edinburgh EH2 3BU; Tel: 0131 220 0093

Wales/Cymru, 2nd Floor, South Gate House, Wood Street, Cardiff CF1 1EW; Tel: 01222 226257

Charities Aid Foundation, Kings Hill, West Malling, Kent ME19 4TA; Tel: 01732 520000

Childrens' Rights Officer Association (CROA), Dunsterville House, Manchester Road, Rochdale, Lancashire OL11 3RB; Tel: Freefone 0800 387809

Citizens' Advice Bureau
Consult your local phone book

City and Guilds of London Institute, 1 Giltspur Street, London EC1A 9DD; Tel: 0171 294 3167

College of Occupational Therapists, 106–14 Borough High Street, Southwark, London SE1 1LB; Tel: 0171 357 6480

College of Speech and Language Therapists, 7 Bath Place, Rivington Street, London EC24 3DR; Tel: 0171 613 3855

Commission for Racial Equality (CRE), Head Office, Elliot House, 10–12 Allington Street, London SW1E 5EH; Tel: 0171 828 7022.

Community Service Volunteers Offices: 237 Pentonville Road, London N1 9NJ; Tel: 0171 278 2390
E. Force Media (CSV), 81–87 Academy Street, Belfast BT1 2BD; Tel: 01232 232621
236 Clyde Street, Glasgow G1 4JH; Tel: 0141 204 1681
Longstaff House, West Canal Wharf, Cardiff CF1 5BB; Tel: 01222 235458

CSU Publications Ltd, Prospects House, Booth Street East, Manchester M13 9ED. Tel: 0161 277 5200

Department for Education and Employment, Sanctuary Building, Great Smith Street, London SW1P 3BT; Tel: 0171 925 5000

DIAL UK (Disabled Issues Information), Park Lodge, St Catherine's Hospital, Tickhill Road, Doncaster DN4 8QN; Tel: 01302 310123, Fax: 01302 310404, Textphone: 01302 310123

Disability Now **(magazine)**, 6 Market Road, London N7 9PW; Tel: 0171 619 7329 for editorial, 0171 564 7219 for advertising

Educational Grants Advisory Service, Family Welfare Association, 501–505 Kingsland Road, London E8 4AU

English National Board for Nursing, Midwifery and Health Visiting, 170 Tottenham Court Road, London W1P 0HA; Tel: 0171 388 3131

Federation of Black Housing Organisations, Basement Offices, 137 Euston Road, London NW1 2AA; Tel: 0171 388 1560, Fax: 0171 383 0613

Federation of Independent Advice Centres (FIAC), 4 Deans Court, St Paul's Churchyard, London EC4V 5AA; Tel: 0171 489 1800

Health Service Careers, PO Box 204, London SE99 7UW

Health Visitors Association, 23 Portland Place, London W1N 3AF

HM Prison Service, Home Office, Cleland House, Page Street, London SW1P 4LN; Tel: 0171 273 4000

Jewish Care, 221 Golders Green Road, London NW11 9DQ; Tel: 0181 922 2000

Marriage Care (formerly Catholic Marriage Advisory Council), Clitheroe House, 1 Blythe Mews, Blythe Road, London W14 0NW; Tel: 0171 371 1341

Useful addresses

MIND (National Association for Mental Health), Granta House, 15–19 Broadway, London E15 4BQ; Tel: 0181 519 2122

NACRO (National Association for the Care and Resettlement of Offenders), 169 Clapham Road, London SW9 0PU; Tel: 0171 582 6500

NARC (Needs, Advocacy and Rights for Children) includes CROA, Childrens' Rights Officers Association, Dunsterville House, Manchester Road, Rochdale, Lancashire OL11 3RB; Tel: Freefone 0800 387809

National Association of Family Mediation and Conciliation Services (National Family Mediation), 9 Tavistock Place, London WC1H 9SN; Tel: 0171 383 5993

National Association for Maternal and Child Welfare, 40 Osnaburgh Street, London NW1 3ND; Tel: 0171 383 4117

National Association for Social Workers in Education, Room 156, County Hall, Surrey County Council, Kingston upon Thames, Surrey KT1 2DN; Tel: 0181 541 9559

National Association of Probation Officers, 3–4 Chivalry Road, London SW11 1HT; Tel: 0171 223 4887

National Association of Volunteer Bureaux, New Oxford House, 16 Waterloo Street, Birmingham B2 5UG; Tel: 0121 633 4043

National Board for Nursing, Midwifery and Health Visiting's regional offices: RAC House, 79 Chichester Street, Belfast BT1 4JE; Tel: 01232 551090
22 Queen Street, Edinburgh EH2 1NT; Tel: 0131 226 7371
2nd Floor, Golate House, 101 St Mary's Street, Cardiff CF1 1DX; Tel: 01222 261400

National Council for Voluntary Organisations, Regent's Wharf, 8 All Saints Street, London N1 9RL; Tel: 0171 713 6161

National Council of YMCAs, 640 Forest Road, London E17 3DZ; Tel: 0181 520 5599

National Federation of Access Centres, Herewood College, Branston Crescent, Tile Hill Lane, Coventry CV4 9SW; Tel: 01203 426146; Fax: 01203 604305

National Federation of Community Organisations, 8–9 Upper Street, London N1 0PR; Tel: 0171 226 0189

National Union of Students, 461 Holloway Road, London N7 6LJ; Tel: 0171 272 8900

National Youth Advocacy Service (NYAS), 1 Downham Road South, Heswall, Wirral, Merseyside L60 5RG; Tel: 0151 342 7852

National Youth Agency, 17–23 Albion Street, Leicester LE1 6GD; Tel: 0116 285 6789

1990 Trust, Southbank Technopark, 90 London Road, London SE1 6LN, Tel/fax: 0171 717 1579

Open University, School of Health and Social Welfare, Walton Hall, Milton Keynes, MK7 6AA; Tel: 01908 653743 or 653140, Fax: 01908 858787

Probation training consortia:
Hertfordshire Probation Service, Leahoe House, County Hall, Hertford SG13 8EH
For north of the Thames

    Dorset Probation Service, Court Building, Worgret Road, Wareham BH20 6BE
For the South West

    Humberside Probation Service, Greenawn, 1, Airmyn Road, Goole, N Humberside DN14 6XA
For Yorkshire and Humberside

Useful addresses

Mid Glamorgan Probation Service, Brackla House, Brackla Street, Bridgend CF31 1BZ
For Wales

Midlands Training and Assessment Consortium, c/o West Midlands Probation Service, 1 Victoria Square, Birmingham B1 1BD
For the Midlands

Probation Northwest Consortium, 1c Derby Lane, Old Swan, Liverpool L13 6QA
For the North West

S E Probation Centre, College House, Woodbridge Road, Guildford, Surrey GU1 4RS
For the South East

Teeside Probation Service, 2nd Floor, Prudential House, 31/33 Albert Road, Middlesborough TS1 1PE
For the North East

For London area: telephone applications only; 0171 233 2024

Probation Training Unit, Room 445, Home Office, 50 Queen Anne's Gate, London SW1H 9AT; Tel: 0171 273 4000

Relate, Herbert Gray College, Little Church Street, Rugby CV21 3AP; Tel: 01788 573241

Royal National Institute for the Blind (RNIB), 224 Great Portland Street, London W1N 6AA; Tel: 0171 388 1266, Fax: 0171 388 2034

Royal National Institute for the Deaf (RNID), 19–23 Featherstone Street, London EC1Y 8SL; Tel: 0171 296 8000, Fax: 0171 296 8199, Textphone: 0171 296 8001 (minicom)

Samaritans
Consult your local phone book

Careers in Social Care

Save the Children Fund, Mary Datchelor House, 17 Grove Lane, London SE5 8SP; Tel. 0171 703 5400

Scottish Association for the Care and Resettlement of Offenders (SACRO), 31 Palmerston Place, Edinburgh EH12 5AP; Tel: 0131 226 4222

Scottish Community Education Council, Roseberry House, 9 Haymarket Terrace, Edinburgh EH12 5EZ; Tel: 0131 313 2488

Scottish Council for Voluntary Organisations, 18–19 Claremont Crescent, Edinburgh EH7 4QD; Tel: 0131 556 3882

Scottish Education Department (Awards branch), Golfview House, 3 Redheughs Rigg, Edinburgh EH12 9HH; Tel: 0131 476 8212

Scottish Health Service Centre, Crewe Road South, Edinburgh EH4 2LF; Tel: 0131 332 2335

Scottish Prison Service, Calton House, 5 Redheughs Rigg, Edinburgh EH12 9HH; Tel: 0131 556 8400

SHAD (Support and Housing Assistance for People with Disabilities), 5 Bedford Hill, London SW12 9ET; Tel: 0181 675 6095

SKILL (National Bureau for Students with Disabilities), 336 Brixton Road, London SW9 7AA; Tel: 0171 274 0565

Social Work Admissions System (SWAS), Fulton House, Jessop Avenue, Cheltenham, Gloucestershire GL50 3SH; Tel: 01242 544600

Soldiers, Sailors and Airmen's Families Association, 19 Queen Elizabeth Street, London SE1 2LP; Tel: 0171 403 8783

Useful addresses

Staffordshire University, Admissions Tutor, Diploma in Advice Work and Law, Brindley Building, Leek Road, Stoke on Trent ST4 2DF; Tel: 01782 294646

UK College of Family Mediators, 24–32 Stephenson Way, London NW1 2HY; Tel: 0171 391 9162

Universities and Colleges Admission Service (UCAS), PO Box 67, Cheltenham, Gloucester GL50 3SF; Tel: 01242 222444

Voluntary Service Belfast, 70–72 Lisburn Road, Belfast BT9 6AF; Tel: 01232 200850

Wales Youth Agency, Leslie Court, Lon-y-Llyn, Caerphilly, Mid Glamorgan CF8 1BQ; Tel: 01222 880088

Youth Action Northern Ireland, Hampton, Glenmachan Park, Belfast BT4 2PJ; Tel: 01232 760067

10 Further reading

Newspapers and magazines

The Adviser (bi-monthly)
Asian Voice (weekly – Friday)
Baptist Times (weekly)
Belfast Telegraph (Friday)
Caribbean Times (weekly)
Catholic Herald (weekly)
Church Times (weekly)
Community Care (weekly – Thursday)
Y Cymro (Wednesday)
Disability Now (monthly)
The Evening News (Edinburgh – Thursday)
Glasgow Herald (Friday)
The Guardian (Wednesday)
The Independent (Thursday)
Irish News (Thursday)
Jewish Chronicle (weekly – Friday)
Job Hunters Guide (Saturday)
Methodist Recorder (weekly – Thursday)

Further reading

Muslim News (monthly)
Newsletter: Northern Ireland (Thursday)
One in Seven (bi-monthly, covering deaf issues)
Opportunities Weekly (Friday)
The Pink Paper (Thursday, covering gay and lesbian issues)
The Scotsman (Friday)
The Times Educational Supplement (weekly)
The Times Higher Educational Supplement (weekly)
The Voice (weekly – Monday, covering black and minority ethnic issues)
Wales on Sunday
Western Mail (Thursday)
Young People Now (monthly)
Youthwork (monthly)

and, of course, your own local newspapers.

Reference books

Bartlett, A (1994) *Where to Find That Job*, Careers Research and Advisory Centre (CRAC)
Education Year Book (1989/9) Financial Times Management
Charities Digest (1999) 105th edition, Waterlow
Voluntary Agencies Directory (1997) NCVO Publications
Social Services Year Book (1998) 26th edition, edited by Rees et al

Useful publications from CCETSW

How to Qualify for Social Work, the Diploma in Social Work handbook, published annually.
Pre-training Experience for Social Work

Assuring Quality in the Diploma in Social Work (1995)
Career Fact Files: Social Work and Social Care
(a) with children and young people
(b) with adults
NVQs from CCETSW
The Work of the Education Welfare Service
Making Connections: Aiming towards a qualified workforce
Essential Information on Level 4 NVQ/SVQ.

Further useful publications

Counselling as a Career (1996) Association of Graduate Advisory Services

Careers for Deaf People, Royal National Institute for the Deaf (RNID)

Careers Tape Library (1997) Royal National Institute for the Blind (RNIB). For free loan ring 01733 370777

Guide to Higher Education and Disability (1999) SKILL (National Bureau for Students with Disabilities)

Jacobson, J (ed) (1998) *The Dyslexia Handbook*, British Dyslexia Association

Moss, B et al (1997) *Disability Issues in Social Work Training and Practice: Maximizing potential*, Prospects, Wrexham

For a good introduction to contemporary social work issues

Adams, R (ed) (1998) *Social Work, Themes and Critical Debates*, Macmillan, London

Index

AASW (advanced award) 73
academic knowledge *see* qualifications
addresses, useful 77–85
admissions *see* application procedures
advanced award (AASW) 73
advice work 47–50, 75
advocacy work 50–52
application procedures
    non- and post-graduate 63
    universities and colleges 60
approved social workers (ASWs) 24
art therapy 34
assessment work 20–21
Association of Drama Therapists 34, 77
ASWs (approved social workers) 24

BAC *see* British Association for Counselling
bail hostels 16, 44
British Association for Counselling (BAC) 53, 75, 77
British Association of Art Therapists 34, 77
British Psychological Society 74, 78
British Society for Music Therapists 34, 78

CABs *see* Citizens' Advice Bureaux
care assistants 18
career opportunities, overview 2–4
Central Council for Education and Training in Social Work (CCETSW) 62–63, 73–74, 78
charities 57–58
Children's Rights Officers Association (CROA) 51, 79, 81
Citizens' Advice Bureaux (CABs) 48–49, 75
civil probation work 41
clinical psychologists 28–30, 74

College of Occupational Therapists 33, 79
College of Speech and Language Therapists 34, 79
Community Care 12, 24
community service probation work 43
counselling 52–55, 75–76
criminal justice system 37–46
CROA *see* Children's Rights Officers Association

Diploma in Advice Work 75
Diploma in Social Work 24, 62–73
disabled people 2, 8–11
Disabled Students' Allowance 61
drama therapy 34
drivers 15
dyslexia 9–10

education welfare officers (EWOs) 26–28, 74
Educational Grants Advisory Service 62, 80
experience, gaining practical 6–7
EWOs *see* education welfare officers

faith communities 4–5, 36
family centres 22
family mediation 56
Federation of Black Housing Organisations 50, 80
Federation of Independent Advice Centres (FIAC) 75, 80
finance for training 13, 61–62

health visitors 30–31
homes for older people 16–17
hospitals 23
hostels 16, 44
housing advice 50

89

Index

Job Seeker's Allowance (JSA)   11–12

language therapists   34

marital counselling   53–54, 76
Marriage Care   76, 80
mediation   56–57, 75
mental health work   24
music therapy   34

NACRO *see* National Association for the Care and Resettlement of Offenders
National Association for Social Workers in Education   28, 81
National Association for the Care and Resettlement of Offenders (NACRO)   45–46, 81
National Association of Family Mediation and Conciliation Services (NFM)   56, 75, 81
National Vocational Qualifications (NVQs)   12
National Youth Advocacy Service (NYAS)   51, 82
NFM *see* National Association of Family Mediation and Conciliation Services
NVQs *see* National Vocational Qualifications
NYAS *see* National Youth Advocacy Service

occupational therapists (OTs)   32–33
older people, homes for   16–17
Open University   12
OTs *see* occupational therapists

personal characteristics   1–2
planning, importance of   13
post-qualifying awards (PQSWs)   24–25, 73–74
prison service   44–45
probation service   38–44, 74–75
probation service officers (PSOs)   41–43

PQSWs *see* post-qualifying awards
PSOs *see* probation service officers
purchaser/provider split   21

qualifications   11–12, 59–76
    financing   61–62
    probation work   39–41, 74–75
    social work   24–25, 62–74

reading recommendations   12, 86–88
Relate   53–54, 76, 83
religious commitment   4–5
residential settings   16–18, 23
risk assessment   21

Scottish Association for the Care and Resettlement of Offenders (SACRO)   46, 83
secondments   61
settings for social care   3–4
Social Services Yearbook   24
social work, professional   19–25, 62–74
Social Work Admissions System (SWAS)   63, 84
speech therapists   34
Staffordshire University 75, 84
SWAS *see* Social Work Admissions System

training *see* qualifications
training consortia (probation service)   40, 74, 82–83

UCAS *see* Universities and Colleges Admission Service
UK College of Family Mediators   57, 84
unemployed people   11–12
universities   59–60, 63
Universities and Colleges Admission Service (UCAS)   60, 63, 84

voluntary agencies   57–58

youth work   34–36, 76